Building Your Tower

Building Your Tower:

Learning the Foundations for Growing Faith

Jonathan F. Morgan

XULON PRESS

Xulon Press
2301 Lucien Way #415
Maitland, FL 32751
407.339.4217
www.xulonpress.com

© 2022 by Jonathan F. Morgan

All rights reserved solely by the author. The author guarantees all contents are original and do not infringe upon the legal rights of any other person or work. No part of this book may be reproduced in any form without the permission of the author.

Due to the changing nature of the Internet, if there are any web addresses, links, or URLs included in this manuscript, these may have been altered and may no longer be accessible. The views and opinions shared in this book belong solely to the author and do not necessarily reflect those of the publisher. The publisher therefore disclaims responsibility for the views or opinions expressed within the work.

Unless otherwise indicated, Scripture quotations taken from the New American Standard Bible (NASB). Copyright © 1960, 1962, 1963, 1968, 1971, 1972, 1973, 1975, 1977, 1995 by The Lockman Foundation. Used by permission. All rights reserved.

Paperback ISBN-13: 978-1-66285-186-5

Ebook ISBN-13: 978-1-66285-187-2

Dedication

This book is dedicated to my Lord and Savior Jesus Christ. He has been my guide, teacher, and King. I pray that everyone who reads this book would be blessed by knowing Him.

Table of Contents

Introduction ix

1. What Is Faith? 1
2. How Faith Has Been Good to Bible Characters? .15
3. Buy Into the Promises! 35
4. How Can Faith Bless You Today? 55
5. How Can We Find Biblical Principles of Faith? 77
6. Learning from the Old Testament Part 1 105
7. Learning from the Old Testament Part 2 147
8. Lessons from Jesus 189
9. How We Can Apply the Lessons of Faith 231
10. The Last Chapter: The Secret to Growth 261

Bibliography 279

Introduction

The inspiration for writing this book is purely obedience to the Lord. For a while, I had known that the Lord had shared with me an interesting discovery that would one day be turned into a book. It was this, that every instance of Jesus speaking about another person's faith was an opportunity to learn about faith. I took up this challenge to study out faith and all the different lessons on faith that not only Jesus taught, but also what the Lord showed me about faith in Old Testament heroes. I had first imagined this book to be a practical collection of lessons that a person could read about and apply to their lives, but it quickly changed from that. Though this book does have many lessons on faith, it also dives into the overall importance of faith in the grand story of humanity's redemption through Christ. I have learned much from many different teachers, Derek Prince, John Ramirez, Kevin Zadai, Kynan Bridges, Chuck Missler, and many other amazing teachers, but the foremost of them being the Holy Spirit. He truly brings me all the wisdom and understanding that can be found in this book. He has shared with me the secrets of Scripture, and I am eternally grateful for the relationship that we have together. The first encounters that I had with the Holy Spirit have actually been in the Word of God. Spending time reading the Bible, I have, many times, received revelation from the Holy Spirit that brings me closer and closer to Him. This brings me to my testimony. For those of you who do not know my story, I was raised in a Christian household and family. Now we were not your typical Christian family, though, because we were part of what you would call the Hebrew Roots movement. We kept some aspects of the Torah, kept the biblical feast days, such as Passover, and worshiped Jesus as Messiah. Now even though I was raised in this environment, I really didn't have a relationship with God.

I think I always knew He existed, but I never really cared too much about Him growing up. I was more interested in playing football. For a long time, football and other sports were the most important thing in my life, I would say to the point of idolatry. But one day, while I was a freshman in high school, my Aunt Dawn was visiting us, and she was raving about the book of James. She asked me if I had ever read the book of James, and I told her I hadn't got to that part of the Bible yet, knowing full well I hadn't gotten to any part of the Bible yet. At the time, the extent of my Bible reading was thinking I should start at the beginning, reading a few chapters of Genesis, and giving up because it was boring (I know some of you can relate to that experience). My aunt then made me promise to read the book of James, and for whatever reason, I actually kept that promise. After I got done reading James, my eyes were completely opened to the Bible. From my experience, the Bible was just a book about some old people in the desert. But after I read James, I realized that the Word of God held wisdom and teaching that I needed! I went to my mom and asked her what book in the Bible had straight teaching like James because I still wasn't interested in the stories. She pointed me to the book of Proverbs. I loved Proverbs, but after reading it, I had a feeling like I should read about Jesus. This was partly because I started to realize how much of the Bible I didn't understand. So I went to the gospel of Matthew and started to read. While I was reading, I got to know about the person of Jesus and His teachings. I fell in love with who He was and is. My understanding of Jesus before I knew Him was that He loved people and died for me on the cross. That was the extent of it. But after actually reading about Him, I realized how good He really was. So much so that in the middle of reading Matthew, I had to stop and pray. I prayed to God that I wanted to be like Jesus and that I wanted to serve Him. After that, I started to read the Bible a lot and grew in my love for God.

During sophomore summer, I finally got baptized and fully dedicated my life to God. It was after this that my walk with God increased dramatically. I was more convicted, and I had a deeper hunger for the Word of God. After a while of reading the Word, I began to become frustrated that I was seeing some amazing things in the Word of God, but I didn't see them in my life. This started me on a journey that led me to seeking the power of God in deeper ways. Through that journey, I have seen the power of God to change me as a person, and I have witnessed prayers being answered. This is what prompted me to write this book. The Lord had been leading me to write about how anyone can experience a relationship with Him and experience the power of God, to not just understand the process but walk through it. I hope this book can spark a deeper relationship with the Father in you because, in the end, that is what it is all about. Beyond studying, praying, and worshiping, there is a Father who loves you and wants you. I invite you into His embrace and care. The parable that I thought best fits this book is the parable of the tower.

> **For which one of you, when he wants to build a tower, does not first sit down and calculate the cost to see if he has enough to complete it? Otherwise, when he has laid a foundation and is not able to finish, all who observe**

Introduction

it begin to ridicule him, saying, 'This man began to build and was not able to finish.'

Luke 14:28-30

Sometimes as believers, we can feel like we don't have a path or enough understanding to build our faith. I want every person who reads this book to walk away with the understanding of how to build their tower of faith. I want you to count the cost of faith and find that you have everything you need to build it. May you be blessed as you read this book.

Chapter 1

What Is Faith?

I am so excited that you decided to get this book and that you have a desire to grow in faith! Now this book is going to cover a lot of topics, and you will read some awesome teachings that the Lord has shared with me, but first, we have to lay the groundwork. We have to make sure that we are on the same page as to what faith really means, so we have to ask the question: "What is faith?" Most of the time, in Christian circles, we talk about having faith, but often we forget to talk about what it really is. Is it some mental ascent to a belief in God? Is it the observance of religious teachings and doctrine? Is it trusting in God and His promises? What exactly is the faith that we are called to in the Bible? Before we can go ahead and look for that answer, I want to take a look at all the definitions in the English language of faith and see which one works best for the type of faith that the Bible characters had. Let's take a look.

There are a bunch of definitions for faith in the English language. We'll talk about the ones that relate to the biblical sense of the word.

Faith (according to Dictionary.com):

1. Confidence or trust in a person or thing

2. Belief that is not based on proof

3. Belief in God or in the doctrines or teachings of religion

4. Belief in anything, as a code of ethics, standards of merit, etc.

5. A system of religious belief

6. The obligation of loyalty or fidelity to a person, promise, engagement, etc.

7. The observance of this obligation; fidelity to one's promise, oath, allegiance, etc.:

8. Christian theology: the trust in God and His promises as made through Christ and the Scriptures by which humans are justified or saved.

Most often, the word faith can be seen contextually as a type of trust. Whether it be the trust in the promises of God, in the sacrifice of Christ, or in the sense that the Lord will provide for His people. Faith isn't some kind of mental ascent to a belief by convincing oneself that God is real or that Christ really died for them, but it is rather a real world application of that faith, a trust in God, so that one can live in freedom from the cares of the world. It is the trust that God will take care of you in all aspects of life; your physical health, your mental health, your finances, your relationships, and most importantly your righteousness. Faith cannot be real unless that faith is manifested into reality by action. Now I don't just want to tell you what faith is, so let me prove it to you.

Abraham had faith, so he left his homeland. Moses had faith, so he went to Egypt when God sent him. David had faith, so he went out to slay Goliath. Esther had faith, so she risked execution to see the king. Gideon had faith, so he went out and fought the Midianites. Shadrach, Meshach, and Abednego had faith, so they chose to refuse the king. Jesus was the ultimate example of faith, going to the cross as a sacrifice for humanity. Faith has always been action; it has never been just a belief. We must come to understand that as Christians, we are called to walk in the power of God by our faith. Now that we have an understanding that the biblical use of faith correlates to the English definition of trusting in God, let me show you all the different places where the word faith is used in the Old Testament.

Hebrew Examples of Faith in the Old Testament

Now there are actually only four different places in the Old Testament where the word faith is used in English according to the NASB translation. I use this translation as I see it to be one of the best word-for-word translations out there, according to my research. Regardless, let's look at these examples. All of the definitions of these Hebrew words are taken from blueletterbible.com.

Example 1:

> *because you broke faith with Me in the midst of the sons of Israel at the waters of Meribah-kadesh, in the wilderness of Zin, because you did not treat Me as holy in the midst of the sons of Israel.*
>
> **Deuteronomy 32:51**

If we do a word search into the Hebrew, we find that the word that is translated to faith in English is actually the word Ma'al. The definition of Ma'al is: to act unfaithfully, act treacherously, transgress, commit a trespass. Now the definition of the word is important, but if we don't understand the context in which the word was used, we can't fully understand the meaning. The context of this verse is that God is speaking to Moses and telling him that he cannot cross over into the promised land of Canaan. This is because when God spoke to Moses and told him to speak to the rock at Meribah-Kadesh so that it would produce water, but instead Moses struck the rock in disobedience (Numbers 20: 9–12).

And because of this disobedience, Moses was unable to enter into the promised land. So we see that in the context of this verse, the most likely meaning of the word Ma'al would be to act unfaithfully. Because Moses acted unfaithfully in what he was called to do, he broke faith with God. We can see another aspect of faith here that not only is it action, but it is also obedient action. It is walking in trust but also in obedience. Because not only do you need to trust God, but God needs to be able to trust you.

Example 2:

> **Will you have faith in him that he will return your grain And gather it from your threshing floor?**
>
> **Job 39:12**

The word for faith in this example is 'aman. The definition of 'aman is: to support, confirm, be faithful. So let's look into the context of this verse. In Job 39, God is speaking to Job about creation. He is asking Job questions about nature, knowing that Job will not be able to answer. He asks these questions to show Job that he lacks understanding and that the things of God are above him. Here is the section of Scripture that the verse was taken from.

> **Will the wild ox consent to serve you, Or will he spend the night at your manger? Can you bind the wild ox in a furrow with ropes, Or will he harrow the valleys after you? Will you trust him because his strength is great And leave your labor to him? Will you have faith in him that he will return your grain And gather it from your threshing floor?**
>
> **Job 39:9-12**

God is questioning Job on whether the ox will do as he says and commands. So we can see that the word for faith in this sense most likely means to confirm or to trust. Can Job confirm that the ox will have brought his grain to the threshing floor? We see that another aspect of faith is trust, but also confirmation.

We need to be able to see the fruit of that trust because God is a God who comes through. Can we confirm that the Father will take care of us? Are we certain that the Lord will provide for us? The answer is, yes, we can confirm that the Lord will bless us through the promises that He gives us and answered prayer.

Example 3:

> ***Who made heaven and earth, The sea and all that is in them; Who keeps faith forever;***
>
> ***Psalms 146:6 NASB1995***

The word that is transliterated to faith in this example is 'emeth or 'ĕmet̪. The definition of 'emeth is: firmness, faithfulness, truth, sureness, reliability, stability, continuance. The context of this verse is that it is from a psalm that was written to praise God. In this context, the best sense of the word faith would be stability or continuance. As in God keeps the stability of reality, the heavens, and the earth. And the God who made both heaven and earth is more than able to keep His promises. We can see that another aspect of faith is a sense of stability and reliability in our Father. Again, pointing back to trust.

Example 4:

> *"Behold, as for the proud one, His soul is not right within him; But the righteous will live by his faith.*
>
> *Habakkuk 2:4 NASB1995*

The word for faith here in the Hebrew is ❒ĕmûwnâh. The definition for ❒ĕmûwnâh is: firmness, fidelity, steadfastness, steadiness. God is answering the prophet Habakkuk, and He is talking to him about the judgment to come to those in Judah. We can see that in this verse, God is making a comparison with the proud and the righteous. It seems that the best definition for faith in this context would be fidelity, as firmness, steadfastness, and steadiness are all aspects of fidelity. But what is the definition of fidelity? The definition for fidelity is: strict observance of promises, duties, etc; loyalty.   So we can see that another aspect of faith is loyalty to the Father. In conclusion, faith is multi-layered in what it entails. Faith is obedient action, faith is trust, faith is reliability, and faith is loyalty. But we cannot make a full definition of faith yet; let's look at the Greek words for faith first.

Greek Words for Faith in the Gospels

In the Gospels, there are twenty-nine times where the word faith is used. There are two words used for these translations, so let's take a look at the Greek like we looked at the Hebrew.

Example 1:

One of the words for faith in Greek is actually a phrase or collection of words. It is the phrase, littleness of faith, and that word is oligopistos. The definition for oligopistos is: of little faith; trusting too little. In pinning down an exact and more precise definition, we would have to go for trusting too little as we already know that oligopistos means of little faith. With the precise definition, we can see that the faith we are talking about here is trust. When Jesus says this to people, He is saying that they lack trust, not a mental ascent to belief.

> ***Immediately Jesus stretched out His hand and took hold of him, and *said***

> *to him, "You of little faith, why did you doubt?"*
>
> *Matthew 14:31*

Example 2:

The second word for faith used in the Gospels is pistis. The definition for pistis is: "conviction of the truth of anything, belief; in the NT of a conviction or belief respecting man's relationship to God and divine things, generally with the included idea of trust and holy fervor born of faith and joined with it." In this definition, we can see that belief is also an aspect of faith. Of course, you would have to believe in something you trust. But our faith has to go beyond mere belief and into action. This requires trust.

As a recap for what faith is, let's look at the Hebrew and the Greek concepts of faith and see if we can come to a conclusion as to what exactly the word faith means. Faith is obedience. Faith is trust in both Hebrew and Greek. Faith is reliability. Faith is loyalty, and faith is belief. So what shape does faith take when we see it through the lens of all these meanings of faith? It looks like a relationship. And that is truly what faith is all about. It's about having a relationship with the Father, the Son, and the Holy Spirit. And it all goes back to the garden of Eden.

How the Garden Is a Broken Picture of Faith

To truly understand the importance of faith and how it is the ultimate way to reconnect with the Father, we must understand the garden of Eden. Now if we deconstruct the situation in Eden and how it took place, we can understand how faith was actually in the very beginning of the biblical story. If Eve had faith, would she have believed the serpent? No, because she would have trusted God. If Eve had faith, would she have gone against the command of God? No, because if she had faith, she would have been obedient to the commands of God. If Eve had faith, would she have gone and even listened to the serpent? No, because she would have been loyal to God, and she would not have given the serpent the time of day. We must come to an understanding that the fall of man came from a lack of faith, and the renewing of man comes from a place of faith in God. Everything about our relationship with God depends on faith. Now that we have seen all the worldly definitions of faith, what does the Bible have to say about faith?

How Does the Bible Define Faith?

In the Bible itself, we find that the book of Hebrews provides us a great insight into faith. With this verse, we can understand better how faith works in our lives on an individual level.

> *Now faith is the assurance of things hoped for, the conviction of things not seen.*
>
> *Hebrews 11:1 NASB1995*

The book of Hebrews tells us that faith is two things. It is, first, the assurance of things hoped for. And secondly, it is the conviction of things not seen. Let us break down both of those definitions. In the first, faith is connected to assurance. To better understand, let us look at what the word assurance means. Oftentimes, assurance means a type of confidence or promise that something will come to pass. So we have confidence that we will receive what we hope for. In the second, we see that faith is connected to conviction. The definition for conviction is a firmly held belief. What Hebrews 11 is telling us is that we are to have a firmly held belief in the spiritual world that we cannot see. All activity in the spiritual world is invisible to our basic physical senses, but we know that the spiritual world exists. Jesus tries to tell us how to understand the spiritual world and, specifically, the born-again experience.

The wind blows where it wishes and you hear the sound of it, but do not know where it comes from and where it is going; so is everyone who is born of the Spirit."

John 3:8

Jesus explains that the spiritual world and, specifically, that spiritual birth is like the wind. With the wind, we cannot see it, but we can feel and hear it. Those who have been born of the Spirit can't be truly seen by the world. They can only be heard and felt. The world cannot discern where the born-again experience comes from, and they are clueless as to where we are going. We are going to God our Father. In the spiritual world, only those who are spiritually alive can have true discernment. If we are born again, we are able to develop our spiritual discernment. So we must develop our spiritual discernment to be able to increase our conviction of the spiritual world around us. Once we do that, our faith will increase, but this will also allow us to have a greater assurance of the hope that we have put in Jesus Christ.

Chapter 2

How Faith Has Been Good to Bible Characters

Now that we know what the definition of faith is, here are some biblical examples of faith to help us get an even better grasp on the concept. Abraham's journey is a great place to start. Now the story of Abraham is remarkable and one that is full of awesome examples of faith. It all started with him leaving his father's house and going to the land of Canaan.

> *Terah took Abram his son, and Lot the son of Haran, his grandson, and Sarai his daughter-in-law, his son Abram's wife; and they went out together from Ur of the Chaldeans in order to enter the land of Canaan; and they went as far as Haran, and settled there. The days of Terah were two hundred and five years; and Terah died in Haran.*
>
> *Genesis 11:31-32*

The story starts out with Terah, the father of Abraham (Abram at this time), taking his family to the land of Canaan. Now on this journey, they go as far as Haran. So they haven't actually gone to Canaan yet. And when they get to Haran, the Lord decides to speak to Abram.

> ***Now the Lord said to Abram, "Go forth from your country, And from your relatives And from your father's house, To the land which I will show you; And I will make you a great nation, And I will bless you, And make your name great; And so you shall be a blessing; And I will bless those who bless you, And the one who curses you I will curse. And in you all the families of the earth will be blessed."***
>
> ***Genesis 12:1-3***

The promise that the Lord brings to Abram is that God will make Abram's descendants into a great nation, that the Lord would bless him, make his name great, and that Abram himself would be a blessing. Not only that, but those who would curse Abram would be cursed, and those that bless him would be blessed. And the final blessing that God gave to Abram was that through Abram, the entire world would be blessed (Gal. 3:16). Now there is some awesome teaching just in this passage, but what I want you to take note of specifically is that God is making all these amazing promises to Abram, and Abram actually has enough faith to leave his family and go to an unknown land. He has enough faith to willingly leave the protection, comfort, and wealth of his father's house. That is an extreme step of faith! Imagine if God came to you today and asked you to leave your home, family, and friends to go to a foreign land. Just stop reading for a bit and imagine what that would be like to completely abandon your life for another.

Not only that, but Abram doesn't have all the nice stuff that we have today. He doesn't have easy access to water. He doesn't have a car. He can't contact his family if he needs help along the way. God doesn't even give him a reference point to travel. He just gives him a direction. So Abram goes to the land of Canaan and leaves his father's house. When he gets there, the Lord has another promise for him.

> ***Abram passed through the land as far as the site of Shechem, to the oak of Moreh. Now the Canaanite was then in the land. The Lord appeared to Abram and said, "To your descendants I will***

give this land." So he built an altar there to the Lord who had appeared to him.

Genesis 12:6-7

Abram goes to a new land that the Lord sent him to, and while he is there, he sees all the people of Canaan. He looks around and sees all these Canaanite kingdoms, full of huge fortresses. And then the Lord says that Abram's descendants will own this land. Imagine if you were in his shoes. You are sent off to a new country, and God appears to you and says that your descendants will own all this land. That is like if you were migrating to the United States, and when you got there, the Lord told you that your descendants would own all of the United States. I mean, that is an awesome promise! So because Abram trusted God in unknown circumstances by leaving his father's house, he was blessed beyond measure by another promise of God. Oftentimes, one promise and blessing of God will lead to another, but only if we continue to walk in obedience to Him. Later on, Abram's acts of faith get even more intense. Let's skip a little further in the story.

Now the Lord appeared to him by the oaks of Mamre, while he was sitting at the tent door in the heat of the day.

> *When he lifted up his eyes and looked, behold, three men were standing opposite him; and when he saw them, he ran from the tent door to meet them and bowed himself to the earth, and said, "My Lord, if now I have found favor in Your sight, please do not pass Your servant by.*
>
> **Genesis 18:1-3**

The next step of Abraham's journey of faith is that he is again visited by the Lord, this time while settled in the land of Canaan. Abraham decides to serve the Lord some food and have a meal with Him. Now while Abraham is preparing to serve the Lord, the Lord asks him where Sarah is.

> *Then they said to him, "Where is Sarah your wife?" And he said, "There, in the tent." He said, "I will surely return to you at this time next year; and behold, Sarah your wife will have a son." And Sarah was listening at the tent door, which was behind him.*
>
> **Genesis 18:9-10**

Abraham points the Lord to where Sarah is, and then the Lord makes a promise to Abraham. The Lord, oftentimes, will point you to what He is going to give you. This way, you can look long and hard at it so that you fully understand what His faithfulness looks like. Abraham had to look at the occupied land of Canaan all the days of His life, knowing that God would give it to His descendants. And he also had to look at his aging wife as he trusted in the promise of God that Sarah would have a son. Now this promise is important because the previous promises of God were based on Abraham having descendants. But Sarah was so old that it seemed it was impossible for her to have a child and thus impossible for the promise of God to be fulfilled. So much so that if you read later on, we see that when Sarah hears this promise, she laughs to herself. At times, the promises of God seem laughable because they seem impossible or too good to be true, but with God, all things are possible. This is a super important promise, and it will bring us to understand Abraham even more as we see what happened to the promised son. Let's skip forward again into the story of Abram, where, at this point, his name is changed by God to Abraham.

> *Now it came about after these things, that God tested Abraham, and said to him, "Abraham!" And he said, "Here*

> *I am." He said, "Take now your son, your only son, whom you love, Isaac, and go to the land of Moriah, and offer him there as a burnt offering on one of the mountains of which I will tell you."*
>
> *Genesis 22:1-2*

Now this part of Abraham's story gets intense. Abraham had followed the Lord all the way out to Canaan, leaving behind his father's house. God promised Abraham that his descendants would own the land of Canaan. He then performs a miracle for Abraham and gives him a son through Sarah, fulfilling His promise. And now God comes to Abraham and asks him to sacrifice his son Isaac as a burnt offering. To Abraham, it may look like God is going in the wrong direction. How can God give Canaan to my descendants if I sacrifice Isaac? How can I become a great nation if I don't have any offspring? How can God give me Isaac through a miracle and then ask me to sacrifice him? I mean, this is what I would be asking myself if I was in Abraham's position. But Abraham had great faith, and this is what he told his servants that went with him to sacrifice Isaac.

> *Abraham said to his young men, "Stay here with the donkey, and I and the lad*

> *will go over there; and we will worship and return to you."*
>
> *Genesis 22:5*

Abraham has such faith in God that he tells his servants that both Isaac and he will go to worship the Lord and return. That means that Abraham already knew that Isaac was going to return alive. Whether that means Abraham knew that a sacrifice was going to be provided or that Isaac would be resurrected doesn't matter. Abraham had faith that God would bring back Isaac. And that is because of this promise that God gave.

> *He said, "Do not stretch out your hand against the lad, and do nothing to him; for now I know that you fear God, since you have not withheld your son, your only son, from Me."*
>
> *Genesis 22:12*
>
> *By faith Abraham, when he was tested, offered up Isaac, and he who had received the promises was offering up his only begotten son; it was he to whom it was said, "In Isaac your*

descendants shall be called." He considered that God is able to raise people even from the dead, from which he also received him back as a type.

Hebrews 11:17-19 NASB1995

You see, Abraham knew that God wouldn't kill Isaac because God promised that through Isaac, his descendants would be named. This is basically saying that the blessing and the promises of God would come through Isaac. Now, if God is faithful, which Abraham already knew due to the fact that his wife was able to give birth to a son in her old age, then Abraham knew that Isaac would live and be raised from the dead. We can learn something about faith from Abraham when it comes to this story. And this is because Abraham knew the importance of covenant. You see, Abraham didn't have the Bible. He didn't know about Jesus. There was no standard religion for worshiping the one true God. No one told him about their testimony of God. So the only evidence and the only thing that Abraham had to work with was the promises that God had made. Abraham had to rely on what the Lord said to him and the answers to the promises He had made. We actually have a ton more to go off of in terms of trust and faith in the Lord because we have so much more than Abraham.

We have many believers out there with amazing testimonies. We have the entire Bible to learn from and grow in our faith. And we have a heavenly high priest, Jesus, who will mediate between us and the Father. We have the Holy Spirit inside of us! We have been given so many great resources for the growth of our faith, but Abraham didn't have any of that. I believe that is why God was so impressed by his faith. Abraham trusted God as a person just as any one of us today would trust one of our friends. If your friend promised you something and followed through with that promise, then you know you can trust them. I know that we all should be treating God in the same way. When God follows through with something, we should trust Him. But for some reason, we have a hard time remembering that He followed through last time. Sometimes we forget to see God as a person. We wouldn't constantly doubt if our friends would actually do what they promised, so why do we do that to God? And God is more reliable than your closest friend or family member. If we can view God as Abraham viewed God, as a person that follows through with what they say, our faith can grow leaps and bounds.

Some of us never put our trust in God; therefore, we never build trust. You have to start asking for things in order to build up your faith because the more you ask, the more will be answered for you.

How Faith Blessed the World

Now that we got a glimpse of faith in action through Abraham, let's talk about how faith is actually the very thing that has brought the world back to the Father, and that is the story of Jesus Christ. You see, all that Jesus did was walk in faith with God. He had so much faith that He walked on water. It wasn't any different for Him than it is for us. That is because when Jesus was on the earth, He didn't walk as the Son of God, but He walked as the Son of Man. This is why Jesus said that we will do His works and works that were greater than His.

> *Truly, truly, I say to you, he who believes in Me, the works that I do, he will do also; and greater works than these he will do; because I go to the Father.*
>
> *John 14:12*

Man is notable to do the works of the Son of God, but Jesus says that we will do His works and greater because He walked as a Son of Man. And because He walked as the Son of Man, He became for humanity the ultimate example and the ultimate sacrifice. Jesus's ministry was always about faith. That is why He constantly talked about the faith of those being healed and the faith of His disciples. The ultimate act of faith that Jesus ever did was when He willingly went to the cross. Now there are two parts to this act of faith. Jesus went to the cross because He had the faith to be obedient to the plan of the Father, but He also had the faith and trust that He would be resurrected. He had to trust that after it was all said and done, the Father would resurrect Him from the dead. Now imagine that kind of faith. Sometimes we struggle in trusting God with the tithe or with giving to the homeless that God will actually bless us as we give to His kingdom and cause. Now imagine you were told that you had to willingly give yourself up and die a brutal death on a cross, but you would be raised from the dead after. That is the kind of powerful faith that our Lord and Savior Jesus had. And that is the faith that we all should be striving for in our walk with God. He is the ultimate example for all mankind in every way!

> *For you have been called for this purpose, since Christ also suffered for you, leaving you an example for you to follow in His steps, who committed no sin, nor was any deceit found in His mouth; and while being reviled, He did not revile in return; while suffering, He*

uttered no threats, but kept entrusting Himself to Him who judges righteously;

1 Peter 2:21-23

For those whom He foreknew, He also predestined to become conformed to the image of His Son, so that He would be the firstborn among many brethren;

Romans 8:29

There is an awesome parallel that Paul talks about in the book of Romans that has to do with how Adam and Jesus share a connection. This is because through the failure of Adam, sin and death entered the world. But through the success of Christ, righteousness and life entered the world. Let's take a deeper dive into the story of the garden to get a better understanding of this parallel. Like we talked about in the last chapter, the fundamental source behind why Adam and Eve sinned in the garden was because they didn't have faith in God. They didn't trust Him. So it would only be right that the very thing that Adam and Eve lacked is the very thing that our Savior had fully, which is ultimate and total faith in God. When Adam and Eve listened to the serpent in the garden, Jesus resisted the devil in the wilderness. When Adam and Eve took from the tree of the knowledge of good and evil for their own understanding and promotion, Jesus gave Himself that we may eat from the tree of life. When Adam and Eve covered themselves in fig leaves, Jesus died to cover us in His blood. Adam and Eve hid themselves in the garden of Eden, and Jesus fully exposed His heart to God in the garden of Gethsemane. He is the ultimate contrast to what happened in the garden. And the main element that Jesus had is that He had a real and trusting relationship with the Father. He had real faith. He had trust.

The Power of Faith

There is an interesting aspect of faith that has to do with seeing something that is there but hidden from view. This may be hard to understand; nevertheless, Let me try to explain through the story of the Red Sea. When Moses approaches the Red Sea with the Israelites, they feel they are free from Egypt. But then they hear news that Pharaoh is chasing them down and is going to recapture them as slaves. So the Israelites start panicking. Because of their panicking, Moses goes to the Lord and asks for help.

> *Then the Lord said to Moses, "Why are you crying out to Me? Tell the sons of Israel to go forward. As for you, lift up*

> *your staff and stretch out your hand over the sea and divide it, and the sons of Israel shall go through the midst of the sea on dry land.*
>
> *Exodus 14:15-16*

What is interesting here is that God asked why Moses was crying out to Him. Why would God ask that question? Can God not see that the Israelites need help right now? You see, God knows exactly what the Israelites are going through right now. In fact, He has already provided a way for them. And He is wondering why they are crying out, not because He doesn't know what is going on, but because He doesn't know why they don't already trust Him. Part of faith is knowing that there is already a way. In fact, in this situation, God actually set up the Israelites to be hemmed in by Pharaoh.

> *Now the Lord spoke to Moses, saying, "Tell the sons of Israel to turn back and camp before Pi-hahiroth, between Migdol and the sea; you shall camp in front of Baal-zephon, opposite it, by the sea. For Pharaoh will say of the sons of Israel, 'They are wandering aimlessly in the land; the wilderness has shut*

> ***them in.' Thus I will harden Pharaoh's heart, and he will chase after them; and I will be honored through Pharaoh and all his army, and the Egyptians will know that I am the Lord." And they did so.***
>
> ***Exodus 14:1-4 NASB1995***

God was using Pharaoh as a tool to glorify Himself before the Israelites. You see, God might cause you to wander around for a bit just so He can use the situation to glorify Himself. He isn't doing this just to puff up His ego, but rather to build trust with you. God then splits the sea and destroys the army. He came against everything that opposed the Israelites and took them out of the way. That is the power and way of faith, that there is always a path that God has for you. But I have another story that I want to share with you that more accurately describes the reality of faith.

> ***Now when the attendant of the man of God had risen early and gone out, behold, an army with horses and chariots was circling the city. And his servant said to him, "Alas, my master! What shall we do?" So he answered,***

> *"Do not fear, for those who are with us are more than those who are with them." Then Elisha prayed and said, "O Lord, I pray, open his eyes that he may see." And the Lord opened the servant's eyes and he saw; and behold, the mountain was full of horses and chariots of fire all around Elisha.*
>
> *2 Kings 6:15-17*

This passage comes from a story about the prophet Elisha in the Old Testament, specifically the book of 2 Kings. Now to give this passage context, the story is that Elisha was being hunted by the Arameans. This was because the king of Aram knew that Elisha was warning the king of Israel of his attacks, and therefore sent soldiers to hunt down Elisha. Now Elisha had a servant, and when his servant woke up, he saw that an army of Arameans had surrounded the city that they were in. The servant warned Elisha of the invading army, but Elisha wasn't afraid. And this is because Elisha's spiritual eyes were opened. He could see all the angels that were ready to fight for him. Now I chose this story to tell you because I think it is a perfect picture of faith.

Elisha had spiritual eyes to see those who were for him. And in a way, that is exactly what faith is.

If we could only see how the servants of God were ready to provide for us and protect us, we would never be afraid. Faith is seeing what has been hidden. It is a path that was always there but that was hidden from view.

> ***Now faith is the assurance of things hoped for, the conviction of things not seen.***
>
> ***Hebrews 11:1***

Faith: The Battle against Deception and the Slander of God

Fundamentally, faith is the battle against deception and the slander of God. The devil has come and infiltrated this world. And his main objective is to destroy our minds and our trust in God. The enemy wants us to be slaves to him. He does this by weaving lies into our lives. The throne of Satan is made of lies. There is nothing real about his authority unless you believe it.

That is the function of a lie. To cause an action or a feeling, based on another person reacting to what they think, is reality. That is how the devil controls people. He will whisper a lie to you and convince you to act on it. Satan did that in the garden. He told Eve a false image of reality, and got her to act on it. You see, Satan desires to be like God; that is what he longs for. But he can't; he is unable to be like the Most High. So he knows the only way to create a kind of Godhood is to make a false reality that makes it look like he is god. He isn't, and in some ways, he is probably lying to himself as well as to us. All he can do is lie. That is why the world is so corrupt and evil. There is a madman running it who is trying to literally fight God, the person who created all things. Take that in for a moment. This is your enemy; this is the person who wants to destroy reality and destroy you. He wants you to believe in all his lies so you do what he wants you to do. Satan tells us we are not loved by God, so that we would seek other ways to find fulfillment. Satan tells us that we aren't good enough for God. He tells us that we should just give in rather than resist the flesh. He makes mankind into flesh zombies that are controlled by desires that he manufactures through culture and technology. What a loser. And yet he would have destroyed us if not for Jesus. Jesus is the truth, and He is the only one who is able to put the lie to death. So He came down to earth and taught men the truth. He came down to destroy the works of the devil. And after He accomplished His mission, He went back to the Father and sent us a Helper. This Helper is the Holy Spirit. And His mission is similar to that of Jesus, to bring us to the truth.

Chapter 3

Buy into the Promises!

I want to begin this chapter by talking about some of the benefits of faith. Now when we begin to adopt things and change our lifestyle for something, we often like to know what we are going to get out of it. For example, many people in the modern world are looking into trying a more plant-based diet, even to the point of taking meat completely out of their diet. Now this would be a big lifestyle change for the average person living in western society. But there are some people who actually try it out and stick with it. When looking at these people, you have to wonder why they went through all the trouble to make a change that seems to not make that much of a difference. But, you see, they made their choice because it actually does make a meaningful difference. Most people who eat more greens live healthier lives. We all grew up being told to eat our veggies, whether that was from our parents or from some athlete superstar on the TV. And faith is similar to this. As Christians, we all know that faith is a lifestyle change that is good for us. But just like switching to a plant-based diet, it is going to take some adjustments. There will be some who know it is better, but they like their old lifestyle too much to actually make a difference. There will be some people who never learned about living in faith and will take something amazing away from this book. But in both lifestyle changes, the cause of them always comes from someone weighing the costs and benefits of making that change. So in this chapter, I would like to talk about some of the promises of the Bible that we can have access to because we have decided to live a lifestyle of faith. Let's get started.

Promises in the Book of Matthew:

"Blessed are the poor in spirit, for theirs is the kingdom of heaven. "Blessed are those who mourn, for they shall be comforted. "Blessed are the gentle, for they shall inherit the earth. "Blessed are those who hunger and thirst for righteousness, for they shall be satisfied. "Blessed are the merciful, for they shall receive mercy. "Blessed are the pure in heart, for they shall see God. "Blessed are the peacemakers, for they shall be called sons of God. "Blessed are

> *those who have been persecuted for the sake of righteousness, for theirs is the kingdom of heaven. "Blessed are you when people insult you and persecute you, and falsely say all kinds of evil against you because of Me. Rejoice and be glad, for your reward in heaven is great; for in the same way they persecuted the prophets who were before you.*
>
> *Matthew 5:3-12*

Starting in the book of Matthew, some of the first promises that Jesus gives us are the Beatitudes. Now, if we look at these closely, we can mark down some of the benefits of living in faith. We will inherit the kingdom of heaven. We will be comforted. We will inherit the earth. We will be satisfied with righteousness. We will receive mercy. We will see God. We will be called sons of God. And when we are persecuted, we will receive a great reward in heaven. These are some of the first promises that Jesus gives us. And these are some amazing promises! Now you may ask how we inherit these things from faith because faith is actually never mentioned in the Beatitudes. Well, living in faith gives us access to these because it is our faith that will bring the character change so that we do inherit these promises. Our faith is how we interface with the Holy Spirit and the Word of God. These two will change us to look like Jesus. We should meditate on all of these promises every day to remind us about what we receive in Jesus. But that is only the start of the promises; there are many more!

> *For if you forgive others for their transgressions, your heavenly Father will also forgive you. But if you do not forgive others, then your Father will not forgive your transgressions.*
>
> *Matthew 6:14-15*

Another promise of the new covenant is that if we forgive others for their transgressions, God Himself will forgive us from our transgressions. Now think about this, imagine that you have two friends. You stole some money from one of them, and the other stole money from you. What makes sense to most of us is that these are two separate events. So when you forgive your friend for stealing from you, it doesn't really make sense that you should also be forgiven because these are two separate events that don't really have relation to each other. But in God's eyes, when you forgive someone, He is merciful and decides to forgive you as well. The most amazing part about this is that the transgressions are not even on the same level! We can all agree that lying to a friend is a lot different than lying to a judge. And this is because of their authority. We are given so much just in this promise alone. It is like if you forgave your friend for lying, and then the judge forgave you for perjury (lying in a court of law). So be encouraged by the opportunity to forgive your fellow man, and then be forgiven by your heavenly Father. But remember that we also have to ask God for forgiveness, not just forgive others!

> *"Therefore everyone who confesses Me before men, I will also confess him before My Father who is in heaven. But whoever denies Me before men, I will also deny him before My Father who is in heaven.*
>
> *Matthew 10:32-33*

I personally think this next promise is super cool! Jesus is saying that if we confess that He is Lord to men, He will confess us before the Father. That is an amazing promise! We have the Son of God as our advocate! Have you ever had a friend or family member stand up for you? Now imagine that the Son of God does that for you when you are being accused all because we stood up for Him when we were on earth.

> *And Jesus answered and said to them, "Truly I say to you, if you have faith and do not doubt, you will not only do what was done to the fig tree, but even if you say to this mountain, 'Be taken up and cast into the sea,' it will happen. And all things you ask in prayer, believing, you will receive."*
>
> *Matthew 21:21-22*

Another amazing promise we find in Matthew is that of moving mountains. Jesus tells us that if we have faith and do not doubt, then we are able to speak to mountains and cast them into the sea! Now I know that it may be hard for you to grasp this concept, and even I am still learning to really accept this truth, but the fact of the matter is that through faith, Jesus has given us immense authority. And the more we build our faith, the more we are able to walk in it. This is one of the promises that Jesus gives His disciples. None of His promises will fail.

Promises in the Book of Mark:

There are many promises in Mark that are also in the book of Matthew, so I will not be repeating those here, but I will be showing you a couple of the promises that are specific to the book of Mark alone. Let's check them out.

> *The disciples were amazed at His words. But Jesus *answered again and *said to them, "Children, how hard it is to enter the kingdom of God! It is easier for a camel to go through the eye of a needle than for a rich man to enter the kingdom of God." They were even more astonished and said to Him, "Then who can be saved?" Looking at them, Jesus *said, "With people it is impossible, but not with God; for all things are possible with God."*
>
> **Mark 10:24-27**

I chose this verse because it isn't exactly an obvious promise. And I know that the main focus of this verse is the subject of the rich man entering heaven, but I want to focus on what Jesus said afterward. He says that it is so difficult for a rich man to enter heaven, that it would be easier for a camel to pass through the eye of a needle. For those who do not know, the eye of a needle is that little hole where you push the thread through on a needle. It is super tiny; not even a bee could get through one of those. Now we all know that it is impossible for a camel to fit through the eye of a needle. So, it would therefore seem impossible for a rich man to enter into heaven. But Jesus says that it is, in fact, possible, but only through God and not through people. This is the promise that Jesus gives us, that all things are possible with God. And if we have God as our Father, what then can we not do with God? To really step out in faith is to believe this one thing, that God is real and all things are possible with Him. If we can grasp this truth, then we will not struggle with faith. Think right now of any problem. Now imagine that problem going away because God can solve it. That is the reality of the situation.

> ***Jesus said, "Truly I say to you, there is no one who has left house or brothers or sisters or mother or father or children or farms, for My sake and for the gospel's sake, but that he will receive a hundred times as much now in the present age, houses and brothers and sisters and mothers and children and***

> *farms, along with persecutions; and in the age to come, eternal life. But many who are first will be last, and the last, first."*

Mark 10:29-31

This verse has one of my favorite promises that Jesus gives us. He says that if we chose to leave all that we have for the sake of the gospel and the sake of Jesus, we will receive a hundred times as much right now! That isn't even talking about eternal life but rather the time we live in today. That is quite a promise! That means whatever you give up, you will be given back and much more! And we can trust and rely on this promise. When God asks you to give something up for Him, remember that He will return the favor and beyond that.

> *And He said to them, "Go into all the world and preach the gospel to all creation. He who has believed and has been baptized shall be saved; but he who has disbelieved shall be condemned. These signs will accompany those who have believed: in My name they will cast out demons, they will speak with new tongues; they will pick up serpents, and*

> *if they drink any deadly poison, it will not hurt them; they will lay hands on the sick, and they will recover."*
>
> *Mark 16:15-18*

The last promise that is made in the book of Mark is actually found at the very end when Jesus commands His disciples on what is known as the Great Commission. He commands His disciples to go into the world and preach the gospel to all creation. He says that those who believe and have been baptized will be saved. He also says that there will be signs of those who have believed in Him that we will cast out demons, speak new tongues, pick up serpents, have protection from any deadly poison, and that we will heal the sick. Those are all amazing signs. This is the promise of faith and belief in Jesus that you will have a supernatural life.

Promises in the Book of Luke:

> *Give, and it will be given to you. They will pour into your lap a good measure—pressed down, shaken together, and running over. For by your standard*

of measure it will be measured to you in return."

Luke 6:38

This promise is similar to the one in Mark about giving up for Jesus and receiving. This promise is specific to giving, though. And what I think is important about this promise is that it is a reminder that when you give, either to those who need it or to the kingdom (tithe), we need to know that we will receive back for our giving. Now our giving should be because we desire to give, not for the gain that we will receive, but because we give from a heart of love. But we should also know that we will receive back because God will always partner with those who partner with Him. He is faithful to return the favor.

> ***Behold, I have given you authority to tread on serpents and scorpions, and over all the power of the enemy, and nothing will injure you. Nevertheless do not rejoice in this, that the spirits are subject to you, but rejoice that your names are recorded in heaven."***
>
> ***Luke 10:19-20***

I think this may actually be one of the most important promises that Jesus gives us. We are called in the Great Commission to cast out demons. I know that a lot of Christians today don't like the idea of demons or even want to talk about it. But if the gospel is true, then demons are real and need to be treated as such. If you believe that Jesus rose from the dead, then you believe that He cast out demons. I don't want to go too in depth on the topic because when it comes to this subject, there are many highly qualified teachers that know more than me. If you are interested in further research, I recommend starting with books by Derek Prince and John Ramirez.

But besides a deeper look into demons, it is important to know that it is a subject that every Christian should know about. From my own personal experience, knowing about deliverance has freed me from many things. I remember one time that I was talking with a buddy of mine about his life, and for whatever reason, I dropped a curse word. This was actually right after I had previously told him that I felt called to do ministry for the Lord. When I saw the look of disappointment on his face, I became convicted. I knew I needed to change, but I didn't know how because this kind of speech had become ingrained in me since middle school and high school. I was asking the Lord to help me, and He showed me that this was actually a type of spiritual oppression in my life.

I immediately went through the process of spiritual warfare, and now I am free! I have also been freed from many other things, such as anxiety, migraines, and even addiction to nicotine. I promise that spiritual warfare is real, and if you choose to ignore or even to not believe that demons are real, you will be stuck with problems that you could have fixed. And these verses are a promise to us that we have been given authority over these spirits and that nothing will injure us.

> *"So I say to you, ask, and it will be given to you; seek, and you will find; knock, and it will be opened to you. For everyone who asks, receives; and he who seeks, finds; and to him who knocks, it will be opened.*
>
> *Luke 11:9-10*

This is one of the most classic and well-known promises that Jesus gives us. For context, Jesus is talking about prayer. He says that those who seek will find, those who knock will have the door opened for them. The promise that Jesus is giving the believers is when they seek something, they will find it guaranteed. Remember this, when you find yourself doubting in prayer, this is a promise that you can stand on.

> ***And do not seek what you will eat and what you will drink, and do not keep worrying. For all these things the nations of the world eagerly seek; but your Father knows that you need these things. But seek His kingdom, and these things will be added to you. Do not be afraid, little flock, for your Father has chosen gladly to give you the kingdom.***
>
> *Luke 12:29-32*

What an encouraging promise! Jesus reminds us that our Father in heaven already knows that we need these things. I think just having that reminder is so refreshing to know that our Father is looking out for us. Jesus had said that we can finally escape the worries of this world. But it comes with a condition; we must seek the kingdom of our Father. But remember the last verse we just read? When we seek, we will find! So if we set out to find the kingdom, we shall. I think this is one of the most important promises to follow because it gets us to the place where we rely on God fully.

Promises in the Book of John

> *He who believes in the Son has eternal life; but he who does not obey the Son will not see life, but the wrath of God abides on him."*

John 3:36

This is one of the best verses when it comes to describing the gospel. This is a promise that Jesus gives us, but it can also shed light into what the gospel means. Jesus says that those who believe in the Son have eternal life. But those who do not obey the Son will not see life, but that the wrath of God abides in him. This means that there is a connection with belief and obedience. And I think that connection is obvious because if we really believed that Jesus is Lord, then we would obey Him. And if we did really believe He was Lord and didn't obey Him, then we are rebels. But we have to remember that if we believe Him, then we will obey Him. And if we will obey Him, then we have eternal life.

> ***Jesus answered and said to her, "Everyone who drinks of this water will thirst again; but whoever drinks of the water that I will give him shall never thirst; but the water that I will give him will become in him a well of water springing up to eternal life."***

John 4:13-14

Jesus promises that through Him, we will have eternal fulfillment. Jesus says that the water that He gives will forever satisfy someone. Jesus is actually referring to the Holy Spirit when He talks about the living water that He gives. I think Jesus chose water because it is one of the most basic human needs. It is a need that we deal with every day. And Jesus says that He can give us water that will forever take away this need. What an amazing promise. We have received from Jesus the Holy Spirit so that we will never thirst again. But what is it that we thirst for that the Holy Spirit answers for us? We thirst for a relationship with God. And when we receive the Holy Spirit, He will come into our lives and never leave. He is the eternal living water that satisfies our desire for God, the very desire that humanity had when we left the garden. We lost our friend and, most importantly, we lost our Father. But finally, we have been given the Spirit of adoption, and our relationship has been restored! Amen!

> *In My Father's house are many dwelling places; if it were not so, I would have told you; for I go to prepare a place for you. If I go and prepare a place for you, I will come again and receive you to Myself, that where I am, there you may be also.*
>
> *John 14:2-3*

Another amazing promise that Jesus has given us is that a place is being prepared for us to enter into. And not only that, but this place that Jesus is preparing for us is the Father's house. We have the privilege to live out our eternal life in the house of the Father. How amazing is that! We, His children, get to have our eternal home in the house of the God. We get to experience all the amazing things He has for us, galaxies upon galaxies of creation.

> *"I have many more things to say to you, but you cannot bear them now. But when He, the Spirit of truth, comes, He will guide you into all the truth; for He will not speak on His own initiative,*

> *but whatever He hears, He will speak; and He will disclose to you what is to come. He will glorify Me, for He will take of Mine and will disclose it to you. All things that the Father has are Mine; therefore I said that He takes of Mine and will disclose it to you.*
>
> **John 16:12-15**

We are promised that the Holy Spirit would be sent to us and that He would guide us to all truth. Not only that, but Jesus says that all things that the Father has are His. But then He says that all things that He has will be shown to us by the Spirit. So if Jesus has all things that the Father has, and the Spirit discloses all things that Jesus has to us, then the Spirit will disclose all things to us! Because what does the Father not have? He has everything, and thus with the Spirit, we have everything. We have no need for anything in Christ.

> *In that day you will ask in My name, and I do not say to you that I will request of the Father on your behalf; for the Father Himself loves you, because you have loved Me and have believed that I came forth from the Father. I came*

> *forth from the Father and have come into the world; I am leaving the world again and going to the Father."*

John 16:26-28

This is the promise of the name of Jesus. We have been given the name of Jesus so that when we petition the Father, He will give us what we ask. What an awesome thing to have! We have the authority to use the name of Jesus to represent us to the Father. It is a similar situation to if you used the name of a political figure to ask for a favor. If you use the name of a person in authority, that can grant you access to the things you want. But only if you know the person whose name you are using. These are the relational benefits we get when we know Jesus.

> *The glory which You have given Me I have given to them, that they may be one, just as We are one; I in them and You in Me, that they may be perfected in unity, so that the world may know that You sent Me, and loved them, even as You have loved Me.*

John 17:22-23

Now I think this is one of the most amazing and profound promises that Jesus gives us. He is asking that we join in the oneness that Jesus and the Father have. Jesus is promising that He is in us, and the Father is in Him. So, in turn, we have the Father in us because we have Jesus in us. I know that this has amazing implications that we won't fully understand until we meet with the Father in heaven.

When we look over these promises, which are far from all the promises in the Bible and even in the Gospels, we can see that a life of faith is an amazing and privileged life. But we need to access these promises through faith. So I want you to meditate on each of these promises as you read through this book. Because by the end of this book, you will have a deeper understanding of faith and how to walk in it so that you will be able to access these promises.

Chapter 4

How Can Faith Bless You Today?

Now that we know all the promises that Jesus gave us, it is important to also look at all the day-to-day ways that faith can help us out. For example, faith is contrary to fear and the unknown. This is because faith is knowing and seeing that which is invisible.

> *Now faith is the assurance of things hoped for, the conviction of things not seen.*
>
> *Hebrews 11:1*

As a mental exercise, let's think of all the ways faith can benefit our lives. Let's start with our relationships. How can faith with God help our relationships with other people? How about having faith when other people lack it? When you have friends or family that are struggling with sickness, finances, or any other problem in this life, your faith is able to help them. Oftentimes, we have people in our lives who need us for support and comfort. If we have an abundant amount of faith, at some point, we are able to not only handle our own problems through prayer, but other peoples as well. This is why we must have faith when it comes to our relationships with other people. For example, when I was younger, my family and I went on a trip to Israel. When we were there, my allergies started to flare up, and one of my eyes became very red. Now this wasn't life-threatening, but it did make social interactions weird as people assumed I had pink eye (gross). While we were there, we attended a Sabbath service with some Messianic Jews. It was a great service, and afterward, we went outside to hang out and meet people from the congregation. At one point, there was a couple who wanted to pray for my family. We all gathered around for prayer and bowed our heads. But during the prayer, the woman praying started talking about healing our bodies. I immediately became self-conscious about my red eye. After that, we left, and we picked up some allergy medicine. I was so happy that we got it because now I wouldn't have to feel awkward! We went back to the hotel and rested for the night. I woke up before my siblings and went to find my allergy pills, but they were nowhere to be found. I was frantically looking around the small hotel room for these pills, but I couldn't find them. I even woke up my siblings just to get them to help. I had lost them. So I went on with my day, waiting for my eye to flare up again, but it never happened. I didn't think much of it at the time, but later when I came back from the trip, I realized that it was the Lord who had healed my allergies! The woman praying for me had the faith to heal me even when I chose to rely on worldly means of solving the problem.

It is also useful to have faith when it comes to our work or career. Oftentimes, we can find ourselves stuck in financial situations that are not the best. Maybe it is because we didn't get that promotion that we wanted. Maybe we weren't able to get that job that we wanted, or even worse, we got let go of a job. But with faith, we are able to get through the financial trials of life. Not just because we trust that our Father in heaven will take care of us, but also because we know we are able to ask for the desires of our heart and receive them in the name of Jesus. Through prayer and faith, we can proactively change how our lives look. This is because Jesus gave us, through His promises, the ability to move mountains through prayer. Jesus never put limits on our prayer, so when it comes to our work and our finances, let's make sure we don't put those limitations on ourselves.

Another area that faith can help us with is with our own personal goals and aspirations. I know that as a person growing up in American culture, we put a big emphasis on being successful, but also in a way that is individual to you. We strive to find success in business or in our careers. But there are two problems with this type of thinking. One is that each person strives to "find themselves," and more specifically, they desire to know what they like so they can begin their journey of excelling in that thing. Whether that is starting a business, mastering a trade or hobby, or engaging in politics, the American culture is to find something and excel at it. People also look for higher reasons for their work. That could look like working for a company that helps the environment or taking the money from your job and giving it to an organization that shares your views. And some people are just content to live the typical "American dream." They want a good job, a nice house, a family, and free time on the weekends to watch football. But just because we have these desires, it doesn't mean we achieve them. And in America, we have a huge market for motivational speakers and self-help gurus. They try to provide inspiration and techniques to help people achieve these dreams. But they fail to realize that real change in a person's life doesn't come from worldly wisdom but from the power of the Holy Spirit. Not only that, but because the world doesn't come to Jesus for answers, they will never truly solve their problems. Jesus wants to teach you to move mountains. So whatever problem that is happening in your life, you have to know that it is smaller than that mountain you can move.

The last and the most important area in my opinion is that faith can help us to change our very nature to that of God's nature. It is the thing that activates the Holy Spirit to move in your life and grow the fruits of the Spirit in you. And this is the ultimate goal of the gospel. Not only did God send His Son to free you from the wrath that was justly appointed to you, but He also came to free you from your sinful nature. That is the main purpose of the Holy Spirit. So when we walk in faith, we can ask the Holy Spirit to train us in those areas of our lives where we are the weakest. If we struggle with self-control, He can fix that. If we struggle with gentleness, He can fix that. If we struggle with joy, He can fix that. The Holy Spirit is the power of God to change how we live. I know personally that in the world, and specifically on the internet, there are so many people who profess to have teachings that can change you. And thousands flock to them for answers to their problems. Yet those teachings will never really change who they are. But it is the power of the Holy Spirit that will really change their lives and their very nature; no more gurus, no more self-help teachers, no more life coaches. The only life coach you need is the Holy

Spirit. He is God, and He has all the answers that you need. His way is higher than any man's way.

Salvation through Faith

If you are a Christian reading this, and I am assuming that most people reading this are, then you already know that we are saved through our faith in Jesus Christ. But what does this really mean? Are we saved if we just believe that Jesus Christ existed and was the Son of God? No, because even the demons believe this and are counted as enemies of God.

> *You believe that God is one. You do well; the demons also believe, and shudder.*
>
> *James 2:19 NASB1995*

So what does it mean that faith leads to salvation? Well, we have to realize that when we have faith in God, faith originates in our heart. It comes out of our spirit. And when it comes from our spirit, it enters our mind, then from our mind to our actions and how we live. So faith is something that encompasses our heart, mind, and body. It translates through everything we do. And when we have achieved this level of faith, where it saturates all aspects of our lives, then we have become fully connected to the vine. That is why the book of James says that faith without works is dead and that the proof of faith is works.

> *But someone may well say, "You have faith and I have works; show me your faith without the works, and I will show you my faith by my works."*

James 2:18

> *You see that faith was working with his works, and as a result of the works, faith was perfected; and the Scripture was fulfilled which says, "And Abraham believed God, and it was reckoned to him as righteousness," and he was called the friend of God. You see that a man is justified by works and not by faith alone.*

James 2:22-24

We can see from these verses that the highest and a perfected faith is one that would permeate through your life to the point where you start to do the works of the Lord. And these works would not be the means by which you are saved, but the evidence of the faith that saves you. So please do not think that I am saying one needs to work to be saved as that is not true. But I want you to recognize that the faith in you needs to grow to the point where you act on it. And this is the thing that saves us from our sinful nature. The overflow of faith in our lives will cause us to live righteously.

> ***Little children, make sure no one deceives you; the one who practices righteousness is righteous, just as He is righteous;***
>
> *1 John 3:7*

How Can Faith Bless other People?

We have already talked a little bit about how faith can help us in our relationships with other people, but I want to dive further in that area of conversation. When it comes down to it, that perfect example of faith for others is Jesus. In every way, He stood in the gap for us and fought for our freedom and adoption into the family of God. But as another example, I want to talk about what Abraham and Moses did and how they, too, are examples of how we are to stand in the gap for others with our faith. So let's go over those together.

> **Then the men rose up from there, and looked down toward Sodom; and Abraham was walking with them to send them off. The Lord said, "Shall I hide from Abraham what I am about to do, since Abraham will surely become a great and mighty nation, and in him all the nations of the earth will be blessed? For I have chosen him, so that he may command his children and his household after him to keep the way of the Lord by doing righteousness and justice, so that the Lord may bring upon Abraham what He has spoken about him."**

Genesis 18:16-19

So this story of how Abraham had interceded for others begins with a story of how three beings, presumably the Lord with two angels, came to see Abraham. I have left out the verses where this happens for the sake of brevity. When these three beings leave after meeting with Abraham, they go off to see the cities of Sodom and Gomorrah. And while Abraham is following along to see them off, the Lord speaks to His angels, saying, shall I hide from Abraham what I am about to do? And He says this question in a way that basically implies He will not hide from Abraham what He will do. And the reason behind this is because Abraham has been chosen by the Lord, and more importantly, he is in covenant with the Lord. And we, too, as Christians have been chosen by the Lord and are in covenant with the Lord. So the Lord will also share similar things with us, just as Jesus said that we are now friends and know what the Father is doing.

> *No longer do I call you slaves, for the slave does not know what his master is doing; but I have called you friends, for all things that I have heard from My Father I have made known to you.*
>
> *John 15:15*
>
> *And the Lord said, "The outcry of Sodom and Gomorrah is indeed great, and their sin is exceedingly grave. I will go down now, and see if they have done entirely according to its outcry, which has come to Me; and if not, I will know." Then the men turned away*

> *from there and went toward Sodom, while Abraham was still standing before the Lord.*
>
> *Genesis 18:20-22*

In continuing the story, we can see that the Lord had been hearing the cry that was coming out of Sodom and Gomorrah. And this cry was because of all the wickedness, unrighteousness, and injustice that was happening in these cities. So the Lord said to Abraham that He was going to go down to see if the cries of Sodom and Gomorrah were true. What I find interesting here is that the Lord says He will go down to see if it true, yet He stays with Abraham while the angels go down to Sodom and Gomorrah. It is almost like the Lord stayed to hear what Abraham had to say, as Abraham was called a friend of the Lord. And indeed, Abraham had something to say.

> *Abraham came near and said, "Will You indeed sweep away the righteous with the wicked? Suppose there are fifty righteous within the city; will You indeed sweep it away and not spare the place for the sake of the fifty righteous who are in it? Far be it from You to do such a thing, to slay the righteous with*

the wicked, so that the righteous and the wicked are treated alike. Far be it from You! Shall not the Judge of all the earth deal justly?"

Genesis 18:23-25

Now Abraham, knowing the Lord well and most likely knowing that both Sodom and Gomorrah are indeed wicked cities, comes to the Lord and reasons with Him. Abraham suggests that it would be unrighteous for the Lord to destroy the city if there were some righteous people within it. And in the verse above, we can see that Abraham set a number to the amount of righteous people that potentially could be within the city at fifty.

So the Lord said, "If I find in Sodom fifty righteous within the city, then I will spare the whole place on their account."

Genesis 18:26

The Lord listens to Abraham and says that if there are fifty righteous within the city, then He will spare them. After that, Abraham continues to press the Lord and asks that the number of righteous required would be lowered until he reaches ten righteous people. This shows the level of relationship that Abraham had with the Lord. He was able to reason and come to an agreement with the Lord because he was a friend of God. And this is the same position that we as believers are in. We are no longer called servants of the Lord but rather friends. The old covenant at Sinai was about service to a contract that if followed, would lead to a blessing, and if broken, would lead to curses. But the new covenant of Jesus, ratified by His blood, is a covenant of friendship. That we would love God because He loved us first. And that love would be the driving force of our work for Him. This is why we are able to connect with God on behalf of others, just as Abraham did. But let's check another passage about standing in the gap for other people.

> ***Then the Lord spoke to Moses, "Go down at once, for your people, whom you brought up from the land of Egypt, have corrupted themselves. They have quickly turned aside from the way which I commanded them. They have made for themselves a molten calf, and have worshiped it and have sacrificed to it and said, 'This is your god, O Israel, who brought you up from the land of Egypt!'"***

Exodus 32:7-8

This passage comes from the book of Exodus, and the scene is set where the Israelites are worshiping the golden calf at the base of Mount Sinai. This happens right after the Lord had given them the commandment to not worship idols. So God is obviously offended by what they are doing and tells Moses that He wants to destroy them.

> ***The Lord said to Moses, "I have seen this people, and behold, they are an obstinate people. Now then let Me alone, that My anger may burn against them and that I may destroy them; and I will make of you a great nation."***

Exodus 32:9-10

The Lord even tells Moses that He would rather make him a nation of his own then deal with the Israelites. This helps you to see the different type of relationship that Moses has with the Lord. But even with Moses on the mountain with God, he stands in the gap for the disobedient and disrespectful Israelites.

> *Then Moses entreated the Lord his God, and said, "O Lord, why does Your anger burn against Your people whom You have brought out from the land of Egypt with great power and with a mighty hand? Why should the Egyptians speak, saying, 'With evil intent He brought them out to kill them in the mountains and to destroy them from the face of the earth'? Turn from Your burning anger and change Your mind about doing harm to Your people. Remember Abraham, Isaac, and Israel, Your servants to whom You swore by Yourself, and said to them, 'I will multiply your descendants as the stars of the heavens, and all this land of which I have spoken I will give to your descendants, and they shall inherit it forever.'" So the Lord changed His mind about the harm which He said He would do to His people.*
>
> *Exodus 32:11-14*

Looking at this passage, we can see a couple of things. First, Moses comes to the defense of the Israelites on the basis of protecting the honor and name of the Lord. Moses says that if the Lord were to destroy the Israelites, then He would lose honor in the sight of the nations. Moses actually says that the Egyptians may say that the Lord had evil intent in dealing with the Israelites. Then, Moses defends the Israelites on the basis of the covenant. He reminds the Lord of the promises He made with Abraham, Isaac, and Jacob, that the descendants of these men would be multiplied as the stars in heaven, and that they would inherit the land of Canaan. So Moses used both the Lord's honor and His promises to His people as a place of intercession.

Now if we also have faith and become friends of God, we can use our faith in God to rely on the promises of God for the benefit of others. But faith comes first because we cannot bless others through what God has promised if we are not blessed by it ourselves through faith. We can also come before God as His friend in intercession, and we do this by coming to God based on His honor. Moses didn't plead for the Israelites based on how "good" they were but based on what it would mean for God's honor if He destroyed them. And in the same way, we can come to God through faith and ask that He would bless others for His glory.

How Can Faith Bless the World?

We know that faith is an integral part of the Christian faith and the church as a whole. Now in reference to the church, I am, of course, talking about the collective believers, otherwise known as the bride of Christ. Now the power behind the church and the perfect image of the church is that it would be a powerful living body that wields its authority on earth. What authority, you might ask? Well, Let me show you what the Lord Jesus says about the church and her authority!

> *Truly I say to you, whatever you bind on earth shall have been bound in heaven; and whatever you loose on earth shall have been loosed in heaven. "Again I say to you, that if two of you agree on earth about anything that they may ask, it shall be done for them by My Father who is in heaven. For where two or three have gathered together in My name, I am there in their midst."*
>
> *Matthew 18:18-20 NASB1995*

If we look closely at the words that Jesus uses in this passage, we can see that the word for loose is actually *lyō* in the Greek. And the word for bind is *deō*. And if we look at other places where these words are used in the Bible, we can get a better understanding of what these words mean for us.

Lyo:

> *And his ears were opened, and the impediment of his tongue was removed, and he began speaking plainly.*
>
> *Mark 7:35*

So in this verse, we can see that the word loosed is used to explain how a man was able to speak after Jesus healed him from muteness. This teaches us that to loose is to set free.

> *And this woman, a daughter of Abraham as she is, whom Satan has bound for eighteen long years, should she not have been released from this bond on the Sabbath day?"*
>
> *Luke 13:16*

Again, we have another verse that talks about the loosing of a woman from bondage to sickness. Now the sickness in this situation is that the woman was struggling with a type of bent back or hunchback. So Jesus frees this woman, but the word for freed here is loose. And with the idea of a person being loosed, it implies that they are bound by something.

> ***Since all these things are to be destroyed in this way, what sort of people ought you to be in holy conduct and godliness, looking for and hastening the coming of the day of God, because of which the heavens will be destroyed by burning, and the elements will melt with intense heat!***

2 Peter 3:11-12

Now in these verses, if we look at the Greek, we can see that in the section "will be destroyed" is actually just Lyō. So from this, we can learn that the word loose can also imply a breaking up of some kind of structure, and in this case, it would be the structure of the heavens. After looking at all these verses, we can conclude that the word loose has both to do with the freeing of something from bondage and the breaking up of an ordered thing.

Deo:

So the Roman cohort and the commander and the officers of the Jews, arrested Jesus and bound Him,

John 18:12 NASB1995

And he laid hold of the dragon, the serpent of old, who is the devil and Satan, and bound him for a thousand years;

Revelation 20:2 NASB1995

Or how can anyone enter the strong man's house and carry off his property, unless he first binds the strong man? And then he will plunder his house.

Matthew 12:29 NASB199

The word bound in these three verses is the word Deō. So we can still see that binding is used in an authoritative situation, where a person of authority comes to bind another person. This is in the case with Jesus and also in the case of satan at the end of the age. We also know that when Jesus was speaking about casting out demons, He said that He had to bind the strong man, the demon that was in the demon-possessed person. So when we as believers bind on earth, we are doing this from a place of authority and power. And when we loose on earth, we are doing this from that same place of authority and power. But we also have to remember that when we bind on Earth, that thing is also bound in Heaven. This means that our dominion through Christ Jesus is not relegated to only the Earth but also in Heaven. This is why we are able to combat our spiritual enemies. This is also the way in which we can bless the world. We have the authority to change the world as the church. When we come together and pray, we can make huge impacts on the world and for the furtherance of the gospel. If we are able to walk in faith as believers, we can corporately come together and solve problems in this world through prayer.

Chapter 5

How Can We Find Biblical Principles of Faith?

One of the most important things a Christian can learn is how to grow their faith. But if one is to grow their faith, they must have some kind of example to follow. This is why part of growing your faith involves learning from those who came before you. Now you can do this by reading books on faith, listening to Bible teachers talk about faith, or you can go straight to the source, the Word of God. For me, a lot of what I have learned has come from all of these sources, but some of the most important lessons have come straight out of the Bible. And this is what the Lord showed me about faith. If you look in the Word, every time God moves, it is because someone was walking in faith, whether that was Moses going back to Pharaoh to demand the release of the Israelites or David facing Goliath. Every time the Lord moves for His people, there is also an act of faith that accompanies the move. And another way to find out how to grow your faith is to look closely at all the times that Jesus uses the word faith. And we will be going over those times in the coming chapters. But I want to equip you, the reader, with the understanding and ability to go beyond this book. I want you to continually press into God and grow in your faith. And in truth, the Lord will show you if you ask, but if you allow me, I want to show you what He showed me about studying these special places in the Word. So let's go over two examples, and I can show you how the Lord teaches me how to grow my faith.

Example 1:

The first example that we are going to be looking at is from the New Testament. This is one of the biblical events in the story of Jesus, where He talks about another person's faith. Let's check it out.

> ***And the disciples came to the other side of the sea, but they had forgotten to bring any bread. And Jesus said to them, "Watch out and beware of the leaven of the Pharisees and Sadducees."***
>
> ***Matthew 16:5-6 NASB1995***

The beginning of the story starts off with Jesus's disciples coming to the other side of the Sea of Galilee to meet up with Jesus. But when they had come over, they had forgotten to bring any bread. When Jesus saw them, He told them to "beware of the leaven of the Pharisees and Sadducees."

> *They began to discuss this among themselves, saying, "He said that because we did not bring any bread." But Jesus, aware of this, said, "You men of little faith, why do you discuss among yourselves that you have no bread?*
>
> *Matthew 16:7-8*

After hearing this, they began to talk to each other about the fact that they didn't have any bread. But Jesus, knowing that they missed what He was trying to say, started to explain to His disciples that He wasn't talking about physical bread.

> *Do you not yet understand or remember the five loaves of the five thousand, and how many baskets full you picked up? Or the seven loaves of the four thousand, and how many large baskets full you picked up? How is it that you do not understand that I did not speak to you concerning bread? But beware of the leaven of the Pharisees and Sadducees."*

Matthew 16:9-11

Jesus asks His disciples if they remember the miracle of the loaves and the fish that He had just performed on the other side of the sea. This is, of course, to remind them that when Jesus is talking about bread, it isn't really a problem for them to not have any. But what I want to show you guys here is that there is a connection between understanding and remembrance to faith.

Why is it that when Jesus tries to explain that, they don't understand or remember, and He says they lack faith? That is because understanding and remembrance has a role in your faith. So how can we learn from this moment? By knowing that faith is connected to both remembrance and understanding, we can then look for biblical methods and verses that speak about these two things. So let's look over some verses and see if we can find any practical way to have remembrance and understanding.

Remembrance:

When I remember You on my bed, I meditate on You in the night watches, For You have been my help, And in the shadow of Your wings I sing for joy.

Psalms 63:6-7

This first verse that the Lord showed me concerning remembrance is Psalm 63:6–7, which talks about how when David was on his bed, he would meditate on the Lord. He would meditate on all the times that the Lord had rescued him. So one thing that we can practically do is remember the Lord and all the times He has rescued us from certain situations. Another lesson we can learn from this is that we should take out time in our day to remember the Lord. I know it sounds weird, but scheduling a block of time just for meditating on all the times the Lord has helped you is a great thing to do. I know that when I am feeling discouraged in my faith, I have a list that I read through that motivates me to keep strong in praying and seeking the Lord. In David's case, he meditated on the Lord at night when he was in his bed. I personally do this in the morning.

> *Glory in His holy name; Let the heart of those who seek the Lord be glad. Seek the Lord and His strength; Seek His face continually. Remember His wonders which He has done, His marvels and the judgments uttered by His mouth,*

Psalms 105:3-5

The second verse that the Lord has shown me is Psalm 105:3–5. In this verse, the author is talking about how we are to seek the Lord and His face continually. But part of seeking His face is actually looking in the past and remembering the works that He has done. Now in this case, I am not talking about remembering the works that He has done in your life but also the ones He has done in the lives of others, specifically, in the lives of the Bible characters. I want you to know that meditating on what the Lord did for the Israelites when He parted the Red Sea, when He saved Daniel from the furnace, and when He saved Peter from prison will help you to grow your faith. The faith that it takes to truly believe the miracles that have been done in the Bible is the same faith that will allow you to walk in miracles in your life. If you know God can part the Red Sea, why can't you see Him paying off your debt or healing your body?

Understanding:

For the Lord gives wisdom; From His mouth come knowledge and understanding.

Proverbs 2:6

So the first thing to know about understanding is that it is from the Lord. This means that relying on any human being for understanding is unbiblical. Though it is true that the Lord has shared understanding and wisdom to many of His ministers and believers, it is important to test any teaching that is shared with you. That includes this one! But the most important thing to learn here is that understanding comes from the Lord and the Lord alone.

> *For if you cry for discernment, Lift your voice for understanding; If you seek her as silver And search for her as for hidden treasures; Then you will discern the fear of the Lord And discover the knowledge of God.*
>
> *Proverbs 2:3-5 NASB1995*
>
> *Consider what I say, for the Lord will give you understanding in everything.*
>
> *2 Timothy 2:7 NASB1995*

The second thing to know about understanding is that if you want it, all you have to do is ask for it. This is because the Lord gives wisdom freely to those who ask for it (James 1:5). So if you desire to grow your faith, you must also grow in understanding. And the only way to grow in this area is to start asking. It really is that simple. There is no secret or special method when it comes to understanding. It isn't about how much you read the Word. It isn't about how much you serve people. It is about asking the Lord for it. Now this doesn't mean that as soon as you ask the Lord, He is going to give you understanding in all things, but it will be a process that you will go through to gain this understanding. I know this because for a long time, my number-one prayer was that I would have wisdom and understanding. My ego liked the idea of being the most wise and understanding person in the room. Funny enough, once I actually gained enough wisdom from the Lord, I understood that I should be praying for other things instead, like the fruits of the Spirit!

> *As soon as He was alone, His followers, along with the twelve, began asking Him about the parables. And He was saying to them, "To you has been given the mystery of the kingdom of God, but those who are outside get everything in parables,*
>
> ***Mark 4:10-11***

We can also see that those who are in the inner circle with Jesus are the ones that receive understanding. This is why when some people read the Bible, they say it is confusing and hard to read, and that is because a lot of the time, it is meant to be revealed by the Holy Spirit. But if we are disciples of Christ and have the Holy Spirit living in us, He will lead us into all truth and understanding. The closer we are to our King and Savior, the more we will have understanding. If we want understanding, we must first ask and then make sure that we have a close relationship with Jesus.

Example 2:

For the second example, we are going to be looking at the story of Jonathan and his armor-bearer. This is one of my favorite stories in the Old Testament because it is an example of radical faith in God. Let's go through it.

> *Now the day came that Jonathan, the son of Saul, said to the young man who was carrying his armor, "Come and let us cross over to the Philistines' garrison that is on the other side." But he did not tell his father.*
>
> *1 Samuel 14:1*

The story starts out with the Philistines coming out to fight against the armies of Israel. Both armies were camped out and getting ready to fight one another. The armies of Israel were severely outmatched by the armies of the Philistines. But here is where Jonathan comes in. Jonathan was the son of King Saul; he was royalty. He would have been one of the most protected people in the battle that would soon begin. But Jonathan decided that he wanted to go over and fight the Philistines across the way, and he only tells this to his trusted armor-bearer.

> ***Then Jonathan said to the young man who was carrying his armor, "Come and let us cross over to the garrison of these uncircumcised; perhaps the Lord will work for us, for the Lord is not restrained to save by many or by few." His armor bearer said to him, "Do all that is in your heart; turn yourself, and here I am with you according to your desire."***
>
> **1 Samuel 14:6-7**

Jonathan again tells his armor-bearer to cross over to the garrison of the Philistines, "these uncircumcised," and suggests that the Lord will fight the battle for them even though it would be only Jonathan and his armor-bearer. That's right, you heard correctly; Jonathan and his armor-bearer versus a whole garrison of Philistines. That is some awesome faith right there!

> *Then Jonathan said, "Behold, we will cross over to the men and reveal ourselves to them. If they say to us, 'Wait until we come to you'; then we will stand in our place and not go up to them. But if they say, 'Come up to us,' then we will go up, for the Lord has given them into our hands; and this shall be the sign to us."*
>
> *1 Samuel 14:8-10*

Now while they are making their way over to the camp of the Philistines, Jonathan comes up with a plan on how to know if the Lord will indeed help them to defeat the Philistines. His plan is to wait for a sign from the Lord. If the Philistines call them up, then they know they have won, but if not, Jonathan and his armor-bearer will stay put.

> *When both of them revealed themselves to the garrison of the Philistines,*

> *the Philistines said, "Behold, Hebrews are coming out of the holes where they have hidden themselves." So the men of the garrison hailed Jonathan and his armor bearer and said, "Come up to us and we will tell you something." And Jonathan said to his armor bearer, "Come up after me, for the Lord has given them into the hands of Israel." Then Jonathan climbed up on his hands and feet, with his armor bearer behind him; and they fell before Jonathan, and his armor bearer put some to death after him.*

> *1 Samuel 14:11-13*

When the sign that they were asking for comes to pass, Jonathan and his armor-bearer go boldly up the hill to face the Philistines. Now the other thing that is important to note is that Jonathan had to get on his hands and knees to climb up the hill to meet the Philistines in battle. That means he was completely defenseless before the garrison of enemy invaders. But Jonathan had so much faith and trust in God that he willingly put himself in a place of complete vulnerability. Now if that isn't faith, I don't know what is! After Jonathan and his armor-bearer get up to the top of the hill, they start fighting, and the battle is going handedly to Jonathan's side. Now without going through the rest of the verses in the story, the Philistines ended up being defeated because of a combination of an earthquake and infighting because of confusion, both sent by the Lord. This was initiated by the faith and action of Jonathan and his armor-bearer, all because Jonathan not only had faith that God could rescue the Israelites with just him and his armor-bearer, but also because he trusted in God when his sign was answered.

Are Signs from God Bad?

I know what a lot of believers may be thinking right now. "I thought looking for a sign from God was bad?" And yes, you would be correct in saying this, but only in part. What matters is the type of sign you are asking for. This is because there are two types of signs, the sign of faith and the sign of unbelief. A sign of faith is what Jonathan used in order to determine if he should fight the Philistines or not. A sign of unbelief is what the Pharisees asked Jesus for so that they may believe in His message.

> *An evil and adulterous generation seeks after a sign; and a sign will not*

> *be given it, except the sign of Jonah."*
> *And He left them and went away.*

Matthew 16:4

These are completely different things. I mean, think about it, how many of you would be able to put your life on the line like Jonathan did when he faced the Philistines, all because God answered his sign? I will tell you right now, it isn't hard to ask for a sign of faith, but it sure is hard to accept the answer. I would only recommend asking for a sign if you have some very strong faith. Otherwise, you are liable to not act on what the Lord has told you and fall into disobedience. Imagine if Jonathan didn't follow through with the sign that the Lord had given him? How many men would have died by the hands of the Philistines that day? And look at what happened when Joshua didn't consult the Lord when he was conquering the land of Canaan.

> *When the inhabitants of Gibeon heard what Joshua had done to Jericho and to Ai, they also acted craftily and set out as envoys, and took worn-out sacks on their donkeys, and wineskins worn-out and torn and mended, and worn-out and patched sandals on their feet, and*

worn-out clothes on themselves; and all the bread of their provision was dry and had become crumbled. They went to Joshua to the camp at Gilgal and said to him and to the men of Israel, "We have come from a far country; now therefore, make a covenant with us."

Joshua 9:3-6

When the people of Gibeon had heard of the conquering of Jericho, they devised a plan to trick the Israelites into a covenant or a peace agreement. So they put on old clothes, old wineskins, and brought old bread to deceive the Israelites into thinking they were from a far-away land.

So the men of Israel took some of their provisions, and did not ask for the counsel of the Lord. Joshua made peace with them and made a covenant with them, to let them live; and the leaders of the congregation swore an oath to them.

Joshua 9:14-15

The Israelites had believed the lie of the Gibeonites and decided to make a covenant of peace with them that they would live. But later on, when they found out that they were, in fact, inhabitants of the land of Canaan, all of Israel was upset. Now this whole situation could have been avoided if Joshua had consulted the Lord. But instead, he acted on his own understanding and was deceived. We, too, can fall into this same error if we don't seek the Lord for counsel, and we can miss out on the plan He has for us. I remember one time when I was seeking the Lord for counsel as to whether or not I should go to a church retreat. I had just met this group of believers, and it was very much out of my comfort zone to go. But after receiving the answer that I should go, I started to pack my bags. When I was on the retreat, I had people pray over me and tell me things that they should not have known about me. God ministered to me through them and encouraged me in a lot of areas that I was struggling with at the time. God blessed me because I had believed in the answer He gave me. What if I had just relied on my own understanding and chose not to go?

So I just showed you an example of what it looks like to study the faith of biblical characters from both the Old Testament and the New Testament. The trick to learning these things, though, is simple; ask the Lord for understanding! I haven't learned anything in the Bible from my own understanding. It has either been from the Holy Spirit or Holy Spirit-filled people teaching me. I have just given these to you as an example of what it looks like to break these pieces of Scripture down. Later in this book, we will be going over more Old Testament and New Testament Scriptures to find the secrets of faith. But we will not be covering all the Scriptures that need studying! That means you have a duty to search out the Scriptures for more understanding, not only in the subject of faith, but in other subjects as well.

The Simplicity of Faith

For many people, faith can seem mysterious and confusing. But, in fact, most of this mystery comes out of how to get faith and not what faith is in reality. Most Christians know that faith is trusting in God. This is why the gospel is so simple and amazing because it is about being adopted by your heavenly Father. He is the one who will provide for you in every way. I think that if we are to understand faith fully, we need to meditate and have revelation on this verse.

> ***and said, "Truly I say to you, unless you are converted and become like children, you will not enter the kingdom of***

> ***heaven. Whoever then humbles himself as this child, he is the greatest in the kingdom of heaven.***
>
> ***Matthew 18:3-4 NASB1995***

Faith is not childlike, but it is about humility. We are to act as children in our relationship with the Father. What does that look like? It looks like asking for everything and not doing anything on your own or without His permission. Just remember for a moment what it was like to be a child, and I mean a very little child. If you look at the Greek word used for child in this verse, paidion, it can actually be translated as little child or infant. So try to visualize yourself as a very small child; was there anything you didn't have to ask for? You had to ask for water because you were too small to get a cup down by yourself. You had to ask for food because you didn't know how to cook. You had to ask your parents for candy or presents because without them, you wouldn't get the things you wanted. If you wanted to invite friends over to play, you had to ask your parents. And if they said no, it was final. Our culture today promotes independence and individualism. But God promotes dependence on Him and conforming to the image of Christ. We, as Christians, shouldn't have childlike faith, which is to say that our faith is to be mature and strong in God. But we should have a childlike dependency on the Father. And I think that Jesus was trying to teach us this very thing in the Lord's Prayer.

His Will, Not Yours:

"Pray, then, in this way: 'Our Father who is in heaven, Hallowed be Your name. Your kingdom come. Your will be done, On earth as it is in heaven.

Matthew 6:9-10 NASB1995

The very first part of the Lord's Prayer is very telling. It is saying that we want the Father's will done on earth, just as it is in heaven. This means that our will and our plans get put on the back burner, or in other words, we prioritize the will of God over our own. I remember when I was really little, once a week, my siblings and I would head outside to work around the house. And my dad would put together a list of all the things that needed to be done that day. Whether that was picking weeds in the garden, fixing broken fences, or building something in the shop, whatever was on that list is what we were doing. And I remember my dad telling all the kids that when we were done with one thing on the list, we should come back to him and ask, "What's next?" This is the same attitude we need to have with God. We, as His children, should be asking God for what is next on His list of to-dos. We should only do what He is doing, just as our Lord Jesus did.

> ***Therefore Jesus answered and was saying to them, "Truly, truly, I say to you, the Son can do nothing of Himself, unless it is something He sees the Father doing; for whatever the Father does, these things the Son also does in like manner.***
>
> ***John 5:19***

Daily Bread:

Give us this day our daily bread.

Matthew 6:11

Now this is the perfect type of a childlike relationship with the Father, to see Him as the provider of the most basic human need, food. Many people who will read this book will probably be in a place where they feel they don't need to ask God for their daily bread. But remember, we are to act as children before God. We should be asking and expecting God to provide for us our daily bread. This puts us in a position of humility before the Lord that causes us to rely on Him more. And if we are asking for such a simple and basic thing, such as bread, what else should we be asking for? We should be asking for everything in prayer, just as a child would.

Debtors to the Father:

And forgive us our debts, as we also have forgiven our debtors.

Matthew 6:12

I think that one of the most important things we can learn from this part of the Lord's Prayer is that we are debtors to the Lord. But remember, if we are debtors to the Lord, then He is the rich lender. Now I think that as children of God, we are to only have one lender in our life, and that is the Father. This is a type of ultimate reliance on the Father that brings us closer to Him as children. We don't borrow from anyone else. That means when you need financial support, you go to Him. When you need anything, you go to Him. And the beautiful part about it is that He lends and then forgives the debt of His debtors, but only if they also forgive those who are indebted to them. You know what that means? Unlimited funding from your Father in heaven! That's like if your bank forgave you of your school loans and mortgage loans. Or if a hospital forgave your medical bills. That's how awesome our God is, and that is also why Jesus tells us this. You, too, must become an unlimited lender, though, as we are to be as our Father in heaven is. This goes beyond blessings but also our sins. If we become indebted to the Lord because of our sin, others can become indebted to us when they sin against us. So let us freely forgive so that we, too, may be forgiven.

> ***But love your enemies, and do good, and lend, expecting nothing in return; and your reward will be great, and you will be sons of the Most High; for He Himself is kind to ungrateful and evil men.***
>
> ***Luke 6:35***

The Father as Our Leader:

And do not lead us into temptation, but deliver us from evil. [For Yours is the kingdom and the power and the glory forever. Amen.']

Matthew 6:13

An important thing to note about the final verse in the Lord's Prayer is that in order for God to not lead you into temptation, He needs to be the one leading you. Many believers find themselves falling into temptation and wondering why God even allowed them to be tempted in the first place. Well, in order to be led away from temptation, you must first be led. That means you go to God for direction in life. This is another way in which we can walk as children before our heavenly Father. We can walk where He tells us to walk. The Father is where we get the directions for our lives, not your parents, not your counselor, and definitely not the internet. So what does that look like? It looks like going to God before making any big decisions in life. Thinking about going to college? Go to God in prayer. Thinking about buying a new house and moving? Go to God in prayer. Thinking about getting married? Go to God in prayer. He knows what is best for us and how we are to walk in this life.

> *For I know the plans that I have for you,' declares the Lord, 'plans for welfare and not for calamity to give you a future and a hope.*
>
> *Jeremiah 29:11*

Most believers have heard or seen this verse before. But how many believers consider that in order to have this be a reality for them, they need to actually be led by the Lord? If we want the plans for the Lord in our lives, we should ask that the Lord not only lead us but also tell us what to do. This is what it truly means to be a believer; it means walking as a child of God. I am convinced of God that most of this life is learning how to depend on Him. The trick is you never have to leave your parents' house, where you get provided for, because you can always be in your Father's house.

> *For all who are being led by the Spirit of God, these are sons of God.*
>
> *Romans 8:14*

How Can We Find Biblical Principles of Faith?

The Bible as a Story of Faith

I think that one of the most important revelations that the Lord has shared with me is that when it comes to the story of the Bible, it has always been about faith. Every time the relationship between man and God has come closer, it is because of faith. Every covenant that God has ever made with man has been initiated on faith. It was the faith of Noah that caused him to build the ark. This then led to God making a covenant with him and all flesh on earth.

> ***I establish My covenant with you; and all flesh shall never again be cut off by the water of the flood, neither shall there again be a flood to destroy the earth."***
>
> ***Genesis 9:11***

It was faith that initiated the covenant between Abraham and God. When Abraham left the land of his fathers to make a home in Canaan and when he brought his son of promise to the altar before God, this led to a deeper covenant and relationship with God.

and said, "By Myself I have sworn, declares the Lord, because you have done this thing and have not withheld your son, your only son, indeed I will greatly bless you, and I will greatly multiply your seed as the stars of the heavens and as the sand which is on the seashore; and your seed shall possess the gate of their enemies. In your seed all the nations of the earth shall be blessed, because you have obeyed My voice."

Genesis 22:16-18

It was faith that led Moses to confront Pharaoh and lead the Israelites out of Egypt. It was faith that emboldened Joshua to conquer the land of Canaan. It was faith that led the judges of Israel to free themselves from foreign occupation. It was faith that kept King David alive while he was being chased by Saul in the wilderness. It was faith that caused Ezra and Nehemiah to rebuild Jerusalem after it had been conquered by the Babylonians. It was faith that led Jesus to the cross. It was faith that empowered the Apostles in their weakness to preach the gospel. And it is faith that will empower you to walk out the path that the Lord has for your life! Remember that the story of mankind's redemption is not over, and you have a part to play in it!

Builiding Your Tower

Chapter 6

Learning from the Old Testament Part 1

Now we get to the fun part of the book, finding out the secrets of building our faith by looking at the stories in the Old Testament! In the last chapter, we went over the story of Jonathan and his armor-bearer. If you liked how that story went, then get ready because this whole chapter will be like that. We are going to look at David, Moses, Joshua, Esther, Ruth, Noah, Daniel, and Gideon. Now there are many more Bible characters that we could study and look into, but for the purpose of this book, we will be looking at just these ones. I encourage you to study more biblical characters to find a deeper understanding of faith. Now, to begin this study, let's start with King David.

David's Anointing

The story of King David starts out in an interesting way. He was the youngest son of a man named Jesse from the tribe of Judah. David lived with his father in the town of Bethlehem, where he was a shepherd over his father's sheep. Now the story of David and his importance in the Bible actually begins with King Saul. You see, King Saul was being disobedient to the Lord, so God told Samuel to find another king amongst the sons of Israel. The Lord then tells Samuel to go to Jesse the Bethlehemite and find a king amongst his sons. After hearing this, Samuel makes his way to the town of Bethlehem and finds Jesse. Jesse presents his sons before Samuel to see which one is to be anointed by him except for his youngest son David, who was out in the field tending the sheep. Samuel looks through the sons, only to find that the Lord tells him that none of these are fit to be king. Then Samuel asks if there is another son, at which Jesse replies there is one more son tending the sheep. David is then summoned and anointed with a horn of oil, which leads to the Spirit of the Lord coming into his life. Now, this is simply the story of how David is anointed to be king; later on, we will look into his acts of faith to find understanding. But I want to say that in the same way that David was anointed, we, too, have been anointed by the Holy Spirit. When we are filled with the Holy Spirit, it is as though we, too, are being anointed into the role that God has for us. So I want you to realize that you, too, have a destiny that is as epic and important as King David, so take that with you as you walk in faith with God.

David Faces Goliath:

Most Christians know about the epic and classic Bible story of David and Goliath. And it wouldn't be a study on David if I didn't go over this story in this book. To start out, I'll give a little backstory on where we are right now in the timeline of David. This is after David has already been anointed by Samuel, and he has been splitting time between lending his father's sheep and playing his harp in King Saul's courts. Now at the time, Israel was in a battle array against the armies of the Philistines getting ready to fight. Meanwhile, David was back at his father's house tending the sheep. Jesse, David's father, calls on David to check on and bring some supplies to his brothers who are in the army about to fight the Philistines. So David brings the supplies to his brothers, only to find that when he arrives, there is a Philistine that is challenging the army of Israel. Now to give some context on the very bold Philistine named Goliath, we have to understand that he was no ordinary man. The book of 1 Samuel says that Goliath was six cubits and a span tall, with a span being half a cubit. Now, if we look at a converted measurement of a cubit, which was a standard length of measurement at the time, it turns out that a cubit is roughly one-and-a-half feet or 18 inches. If we do the math, Goliath was roughly nine feet nine inches tall. This was a massive warrior who was coming against the armies of Israel. Goliath's proposed challenge was that there would be a duel of champions, one from the army of Israel and one from the Philistines. Goliath was the champion of the Philistines, and he was calling out for a challenger from Israel. If Goliath wins, then Israel becomes the servants of the Philistines, and if the champion of Israel wins, the Philistines would have to serve Israel.

After David hears this challenge, he responds to it in a way that is very telling of his faith.

> **Then David spoke to the men who were standing by him, saying, "What will be done for the man who kills this Philistine and takes away the reproach from Israel? For who is this uncircumcised Philistine, that he should taunt the armies of the living God?"**
>
> **1 Samuel 17:26**

Now that is some confidence! David looks at the giant warrior challenging the armies of Israel and asks why he is even talking. If we look carefully, we can see that David has this attitude because he knows Goliath isn't in a covenant with God. That is why he calls Goliath an uncircumcised Philistine. David looks down on Goliath in the spiritual, even though Goliath would literally look down on David in the physical. And this is because David knows that he isn't just fighting for himself but for God. This is the first lesson that we can learn from David, that just like him, we, too, are on the side of the Lord. David had perspective on the situation because he let God take him higher. Goliath may have been a giant in the physical, but David was a giant in the spiritual. When we are walking in faith, we have to have our foundation in understanding who we are in covenant with. We are in a covenant with Almighty God, the creator and master of the universe. There is no one higher in authority and power than God. Make sure your foundation is this understanding. But how exactly did David have this confidence in the Lord? Why didn't anyone else have the same confidence as David? Well, we actually get to know the secret about how David got this revelation of who he is fighting for. After word gets out that David has some strong words for Goliath, King Saul summons him to his tent. When David arrives, he tells King Saul that he will face the giant. But King Saul doesn't believe in him. Saul tells David that he is unable to face Goliath because he, David, is only a youth, and Goliath is a seasoned warrior. After hearing this, David then tries to defend himself by letting the king know of his past exploits.

> *But David said to Saul, "Your servant was tending his father's sheep. When a lion or a bear came and took a lamb from the flock, I went out after him and attacked him, and rescued it from his mouth; and when he rose up against me, I seized him by his beard and struck him and killed him. Your servant has killed both the lion and the bear; and this uncircumcised Philistine will be like one of them, since he has taunted the armies of the living God." And David said, "The Lord who delivered me from the paw of the lion and from the paw of the bear, He will deliver me from the hand of this Philistine." And Saul said to David, "Go, and may the Lord be with you."*
>
> *1 Samuel 17:34-37*

After hearing this, Saul allows David to face Goliath. What we get out of this passage is insight as to why David had so much confidence in the Lord.

It is because he had already had many experiences in the past where the Lord blessed him with strength. And in the same way, the Lord will bring you situations in life to prepare you for your Goliath. Faith grows step by step. This is an aspect of growing faith that we need to remember. It isn't an instantaneous thing; it takes time, and it takes leaning into the Lord. Now that David got the green light to fight Goliath, let's see what happens next.

> ***David girded his sword over his armor and tried to walk, for he had not tested them. So David said to Saul, "I cannot go with these, for I have not tested them." And David took them off. He took his stick in his hand and chose for himself five smooth stones from the brook, and put them in the shepherd's bag which he had, even in his pouch, and his sling was in his hand; and he approached the Philistine.***
>
> ***1 Samuel 17:39-40***

Before King Saul sent David off to face Goliath, he decided to lend David his armor and weapons. But David decided that he could not wear Saul's armor because he had not tested it, or in other words, he was not used to Saul's armor. So David takes off the armor and goes to grab five stones from the brook nearby. David has decided to wear the clothing and have the tools of a shepherd. What's interesting to note is that when David went to face Goliath, he didn't have to change. God had already prepared him for the fight as a shepherd. And in the same way, God has already given you the equipment you need to face your Goliath. Your situation in life, no matter how small, is being used by God to equip you to face a giant. Now that David had all that he needed, his sling and five stones, he headed toward the battle.

> *The Philistine said to David, "Am I a dog, that you come to me with sticks?" And the Philistine cursed David by his gods. The Philistine also said to David, "Come to me, and I will give your flesh to the birds of the sky and the beasts of the field."*
>
> **1 Samuel 17:43-44**

As David approaches the battlefield, Goliath starts talking down to him. He starts cursing David and telling him how he will kill David and give his flesh to the birds of the sky and beasts of the field. But David has a response.

Then David said to the Philistine, "You come to me with a sword, a spear, and a javelin, but I come to you in the name of the Lord of hosts, the God of the armies of Israel, whom you have taunted. This day the Lord will deliver you up into my hands, and I will strike you down and remove your head from you. And I will give the dead bodies of the army of the Philistines this day to the birds of the sky and the wild beasts of the earth, that all the earth may know that there is a God in Israel, and that all this assembly may know that the Lord does not deliver by sword or by spear; for the battle is the Lord's and He will give you into our hands."

1 Samuel 17:45-47

The very first thing that David does is he brings the battle from a physical place to a spiritual place. He calls out Goliath's sword, spear, and javelin and then tells Goliath that he comes in the name of God. Recognize how David doesn't tell Goliath that he comes with a sling but that he
comes in the name of the Lord of Hosts. In the same way, don't let your physical equipment

determine how you fight, whether that be your financial situation, how you look, or your material circumstances. You are to come to the fight with the name of Jesus. After that, David starts to tell Goliath what he will do to him. He lets Goliath know that he will be defeated and that he will have his head removed. We, too, need to speak to our giants in this way. Part of faith is speaking about what will happen in your life. This gives glory to God because the truth about God is that His Word never returns void.

> ***So will My word be which goes forth from My mouth; It will not return to Me empty, Without accomplishing what I desire, And without succeeding in the matter for which I sent it.***
>
> ***Isaiah 55:11***

If we speak with the name of Jesus, we become ambassadors for Him. And our words go forth as though they were from Him. And we know that nothing that comes from His mouth comes back void. I actually had my girlfriend read the rough draft of this book. And after she read this chapter, she took this in faith and ran with it. When we were at my parents' house, we went out to see the sheep they had. At the time, they were pregnant, but they weren't at the right time to give birth. When I told my girlfriend this, she was so excited but also disappointed that she wouldn't see a baby sheep for a while. But while we were down by the sheep, she reminded me of this truth, that if we pray in Jesus's name, we can have anything we pray for in faith. So she pointed to a sheep and said, "In Jesus's name, have a baby." And nothing happened. After this, we went on a walk, but when we came back, we got to see a miracle. My little sister and her friend ran up to us from the sheep pen, telling us about how a baby lamb was born! Jesus can do amazing things.

So speak to the giant in your life, and let God be glorified when it falls. The last thing that David does is he lets Goliath know that when he is defeated, it will be for the purpose of showing that the Lord is responsible for the victory, and the glory is His. This is the kind of attitude that we should have. If we are praying for promotion and victory, we need to make sure that the Lord is the one receiving the glory. And it is rightfully His because, without Him, you could do nothing. In the physical, David would never have defeated Goliath, but because of God, he walked away victorious. The last thing that I want to say is that we should look at the weapon that David used as a way to understand prayer. David slew Goliath with a sling. It doesn't look like much, but in the right hands, it can be deadly. Prayer is the same way.

Never look down on prayer because even though it doesn't seem like much, it can take down giants. That is all that we are going to cover for King David in this chapter. There are many more things to study from David's life, and I encourage you to take the time to ask the Lord for wisdom concerning them. But for now, we will move on to another character, Moses.

Moses and the Burning Bush:

Now most of us know about the story of Moses and the Israelites' exodus out of Egypt. Moses was a man of God who had a very close relationship with the Lord. So much so that he actually spoke to Him face to face. But I want to look back at a time when Moses wasn't as faithful, and he didn't have a strong relationship with God. We can learn from Moses's mistakes as well as his successes. Let's start by giving some backstory on the life of Moses. Moses was a child born from the tribe of Levi, and his birth was marked by tragedy. At the time of Moses's birth, Pharaoh had given an order to kill all the male babies born from Israel because he feared their growing strength.

> ***Then Pharaoh commanded all his people, saying, "Every son who is born***

> ***you are to cast into the Nile, and every daughter you are to keep alive."***

Exodus 1:22

Moses was born during this time, and his mother was able to save him through a miracle. Moses was placed in a basket on the Nile, where he floated off, only to be grabbed by Pharaoh's daughter. Now Pharaoh's daughter had pity on Moses and decided to take him with her. Moses's sister had been watching this all happen and called out to Pharaoh's daughter, asking if she would like to have a nurse for the child. She accepted, and Moses's sister went to get her mother to be Moses's nurse. Moses was adopted into the house of Pharaoh, and later, when he was older, lived in Pharaoh's house, where he was brought up as an educated and privileged man. Though, when he grew older, he had a longing to free his Hebrew brethren. This longing grew so much that when he found an Egyptian beating a Hebrew man, he killed him, hiding the Egyptian in the sand. Word of this brash action came out, and Moses had to flee Egypt, leaving behind his life of luxury for the deserts of Midian. After years of living in the desert, Moses finds himself shepherding the sheep of his father-in-law Jethro. While doing this, he comes upon an interesting sight, a bush that is caught on fire yet is not being consumed.

> *The angel of the Lord appeared to him in a blazing fire from the midst of a bush; and he looked, and behold, the bush was burning with fire, yet the bush was not consumed. So Moses said, "I must turn aside now and see this marvelous sight, why the bush is not burned up." When the Lord saw that he turned aside to look, God called to him from the midst of the bush and said, "Moses, Moses!" And he said, "Here I am."*
>
> *Exodus 3:2-4*

As Moses approaches the bush, the Lord speaks to him and tells him to take off his sandals because it is holy ground. The Lord tells Moses that He has seen the oppression of His people and that He intends to set them free. He then commissions Moses to be the one to lead Israel out of Egypt.

> *Therefore, come now, and I will send you to Pharaoh, so that you may bring My people, the sons of Israel, out of*

Egypt." But Moses said to God, "Who am I, that I should go to Pharaoh, and that I should bring the sons of Israel out of Egypt?"

Exodus 3:10-11

Moses's first response after hearing the task that is assigned to him is to question why the Lord picked him. Moses was so humbled from the years in the desert and having left a place of royalty to becoming a shepherd that he couldn't see himself doing this. And I would say that many people today have a mission that the Lord wants to give them, but they don't believe they are ready for it. If Moses had his way, he would have never gone to free Israel. Don't let the doubt in your heart rob you from what God has for you. And the plan that God has isn't just for you, but others are depending on you to obey God and follow through with the mission. Just as the Israelites needed Moses to be obedient, others are waiting on you to obey. Trust God that He picked you for the right reasons. After the Lord spoke to Moses about the mission that he was about to go on, He let Moses know that Pharaoh would not let the people of Israel go on his own accord.

They will pay heed to what you say; and you with the elders of Israel will come to the king of Egypt and you will say to him, 'The Lord, the God of the Hebrews, has met with us. So now, please, let us go a three days' journey into the wilderness, that we may sacrifice to the Lord our God.' But I know that the king of Egypt will not permit you to go, except under compulsion.

Exodus 3:18-19

God is sending Moses to talk to Pharaoh, knowing that Pharaoh will not let the people go until he reaches a breaking point. Why would God do this? It is because God often works in ways where we have to continue to ask for what we desire. And it may be that the enemy won't

Let us have a breakthrough unless it is under compulsion. God has shown me that a lot of times, it is about having perseverance. Moses had that when he continually went to Pharaoh to ask that the Israelites be allowed to worship God. Now the interesting part to note is that at first, all Moses was asking for was to go out on a three-day journey to sacrifice to God. But if we read further, we can see what that turned into after Pharaoh kept denying him.

So I will stretch out My hand and strike Egypt with all My miracles which I shall do in the midst of it; and after that he will let you go. I will grant this people favor in the sight of the Egyptians; and it shall be that when you go, you will not go empty-handed. But every woman shall ask of her neighbor and the woman who lives in her house, articles of silver and articles of gold, and clothing; and you will put them on your sons and daughters. Thus you will plunder the Egyptians."

Exodus 3:20-22

What was at first a trip in the desert to worship God turned into a plundering of Egypt and the permanent exodus of the Israelites. This is how God works. If the enemy keeps denying you what is rightfully yours, God is going to make it worse for him. Keep this in mind when you are praying for a breakthrough. The longer it takes, the more the enemy is going to pay for holding your blessing back. Later on, Moses talks to the Lord about how the Israelites may not believe him when he comes to Egypt. The Lord gives him a sign that he may perform to convince the Israelites of his mission. Now there are three signs that the Lord gives Moses, but I want to talk about the first one.

> *Then Moses said, "What if they will not believe me or listen to what I say? For they may say, 'The Lord has not appeared to you.'" The Lord said to him, "What is that in your hand?" And he said, "A staff." Then He said, "Throw it on the ground." So he threw it on the ground, and it became a serpent; and Moses fled from it.*
>
> *Exodus 4:1-3*

The first sign that the Lord gives Moses is to throw his staff down, and it would become a snake. Now there are a couple of things that the Holy Spirit showed me about this situation that are very interesting. The first being that the Lord used Moses's shepherd staff to perform this miracle. This was the tool that Moses used every day while he was in the wilderness of Midian. So God will use tools that you already have to perform miracles in your life. And He can use them when you are sent on your mission. It is important to know that if God has called you, then you already have the tools you need for your mission. The other thing to notice, though, is that when the staff was thrown down and turned into a snake, Moses fled from it. The staff that you have been given may turn into a snake when God tells you to throw it down. If that happens, you are called to something greater. Don't flee from your destiny and the plan that God has for you. It may seem scary that what once was a simple talent or skill in your life turns out to be a powerful tool for God, but you need to be brave and grab that serpent by the tail. Now after all that Moses has seen and been told to him by the Lord, Moses protests that he is not fit for the job. He says that it is because he isn't good at talking, telling the Lord that he is slow of speech and slow of tongue.

> ***Then Moses said to the Lord, "Please, Lord, I have never been eloquent, neither recently nor in time past, nor since You have spoken to Your servant; for I am slow of speech and slow of tongue." The Lord said to him, "Who has made man's mouth? Or who makes him mute or deaf, or seeing or blind? Is it not I, the Lord? Now then go, and I, even I, will be with your mouth, and teach you what you are to say."***
>
> ***Exodus 4:10-12***

So while Moses was trying to get himself out of a job, the Lord told him the truth. He told Moses that it was He who made the tongue and the mouth. That it is by His power man is mute, deaf, seeing, or blind. And this is what I want you to understand from this story, that God is the one who defines you, not the devil and not man. If God tells you that you are healed, then you are healed. If God tells you that you are faithful, then you are faithful. He has the last say and the final word when it comes to the lives of humans. Let God define who you are! The last thing that the Lord gives Moses to help him with his fear is that He gives him Aaron.

> *Now then go, and I, even I, will be with your mouth, and teach you what you are to say." But he said, "Please, Lord, now send the message by whomever You will." Then the anger of the Lord burned against Moses, and He said, "Is there not your brother Aaron the Levite? I know that he speaks fluently. And moreover, behold, he is coming out to meet you; when he sees you, he will be glad in his heart.*
>
> **Exodus 4:12-14**

The Lord will bring people in your life to help you with your destiny. This is why having a community of believers around you is so important.

Joshua and the Walls of Jericho

I know that this section is titled, "Joshua and the Walls of Jericho," but I want to talk about Rahab before we go in depth on Joshua. I put Rahab in this section because she is part of Joshua's first conquest of the land of Canaan. Now let's go over a little backstory before we begin. Moses has just died, and Joshua has now been appointed as the leader of Israel. He decides that before the Israelites are to cross the Jordan and go over to conquer Canaan, he is going to send some spies to see the city of Jericho. The spies cross over to the Canaan and decide to visit Jericho to see if the people fear the Israelites. While there, they stop by the house of the harlot Rahab. While they are in this house, the king of Jericho hears that they are in his city and sends guards to find them. They come to the house of Rahab and question her as to where the spies might be. She tells them that they indeed came to her house but have already left. This, of course, is a lie, and she, in fact, hid the men on her roof under the stalks of flax. After the guards leave, she brings the men back down and starts to speak with them.

> *and said to the men, "I know that the Lord has given you the land, and that the terror of you has fallen on us, and that all the inhabitants of the land have melted away before you. For we have heard how the Lord dried up the water of the Red Sea before you when you came out of Egypt, and what you did to the two kings of the Amorites who were beyond the Jordan, to Sihon and Og, whom you utterly destroyed.*
>
> *Joshua 2:9-10*

This is the first sign of Rahab's faith. She tells the men that after hearing the report about the parting of the Red Sea and the conquering of the two kings, she is convinced that the Israelites have already won. Fundamentally, this is what faith is all about. It is about hearing and believing. But Rahab goes further. You see, she believes so much that she hides the men from the guards of the city. Now imagine if she turned them in? What kind of reward or honor would she get from the king of Jericho? But instead of turning them in, she decides to partner with them and risks her life.

> *Now therefore, please swear to me by the Lord, since I have dealt kindly with you, that you also will deal kindly with my father's household, and give me a pledge of truth, and spare my father and my mother and my brothers and my sisters, with all who belong to them, and deliver our lives from death."*
>
> ***Joshua 2:12-13***

Rahab then asks the men for a pledge so that when the Israelites come to destroy the city of Jericho, they will not touch the house of Rahab.

> *Then she let them down by a rope through the window, for her house was on the city wall, so that she was living on the wall. She said to them, "Go to the hill country, so that the pursuers will not happen upon you, and hide yourselves there for three days until the pursuers return. Then afterward you may go on your way."*
>
> ***Joshua 2:15-16***

She then helps the men again by letting them down from her window by a rope. She tells them what they must do in order to escape the king's men. The men appreciate this and give Rahab the pledge that she desires.

> ***unless, when we come into the land, you tie this cord of scarlet thread in the window through which you let us down, and gather to yourself into the house your father and your mother and your brothers and all your father's household. It shall come about that anyone who goes out of the doors of your house into the street, his blood shall be on his own head, and we shall be free; but anyone who is with you in the house, his blood shall be on our head if a hand is laid on him.***
>
> ***Joshua 2:18-19***

Now we get to the good part. The men tell Rahab that the sign for this salvation in the upcoming conquest is that she is to put a scarlet thread on the same window that they were let down. And the other requirement was that if anyone of the family of Rahab leaves the house, it would be their fault if they got killed. But if anyone of her family got killed while in the house, it would be the fault of the Israelites. So I want to talk about the symbolism here. Just as Rahab and her family are protected by the scarlet thread on her window, we, too, are protected by the scarlet blood of Christ. And if we leave the house of Christ, we, too, have our blood on our own heads.

Now this whole agreement was all made because Rahab had faith in the word that she heard and acted on it. Just as we, too, have faith in the gospel of Christ, so we act on it. The lesson that we can learn from Rahab is that sometimes faith is really as simple as hearing, believing, and acting according to what you have heard. Rahab made the wise decision to partner with the Israelites, just as all believers have made the wise decision to follow Christ. To believe in Him is to enter into a covenant with Him. If you hear from God that He wants you to move to another city, it would be wise of you to start packing. If He wants you to marry someone, start saving for that ring! If He wants you to start a ministry, start praying that He would equip you to be a pastor over a church or in any other capacity that He calls you. Act on the thing that He has told you and watch Him make you look good.

> ***Now He who establishes us with you in Christ and anointed us is God, who***

> *also sealed us and gave us the Spirit in our hearts as a pledge.*
>
> *2 Corinthians 1:21-22*

We have the pledge of the Holy Spirit, just as Rahab had the pledge of the scarlet thread, and we will be hidden in the house of the Lord as Rahab was hidden in her house.

> *For in the day of trouble He will conceal me in His tabernacle; In the secret place of His tent He will hide me; He will lift me up on a rock.*
>
> *Psalms 27:5*

Jesus is the rock that we are lifted up on! We are in the tabernacle of the Lord when we enter into a covenant with Him. But now that we have gone over the prophetic symbolism and the teachings of faith that we can learn from Rahab, let's go over the story of Joshua.

> *And the priests who carried the ark of the covenant of the Lord stood firm on dry ground in the middle of the Jordan while all Israel crossed on dry*

> **ground, until all the nation had finished crossing the Jordan.**
>
> **Joshua 3:17**

After getting the report back from the spies who went to Jericho, Joshua sets out with the armies of Israel to take the promised land. The priest carries the ark of the covenant through the Jordan River, where God holds back the waters of the river so the people can cross over. As Joshua reached Jericho an angel of the Lord appeared to him and gave him the instructions for conquering Jericho. He told him to send the ark of the Lord with an army and seven priests to circle the city, all the while the priests were to blow seven trumpets. They would do this for six days, one time around the city, blowing the trumpets with the army and the ark. And on the seventh day, they would go around the city seven times while blowing the trumpets. The whole time that the army was circling the city, they were also commanded not to make a noise. So the Israelites did this, circling for six days, and on the seventh, they circled seven times. On the seventh time around, the people were given the command to shout, and the walls of Jericho were brought down. The army of Israel destroyed every living thing except for Rahab and her family. They were spared for helping the spies that had previously come into Jericho.

If we look at this story, we can see something amazing. What the Lord has shown me is that this is an image of prayer. Though it looked like nothing in the natural, it was something extremely powerful in the spiritual. The king of Jericho must have thought that the Israelites were a bunch of lunatics for circling his city without doing anything for six days. And that is how prayer might look outwardly, that it would never make sense that God could answer our prayers, but He is preparing you for something miraculous. He wants to give you so much victory that the walls of your enemies come down before you have even started the battle. We can see how our time in prayer is the same thing as the armies of Israel marching around the city of Jericho, preparing for the walls to fall. If we can grasp this as a church, we will be able to withstand the waiting that accompanies prayer. At this point in my prayer life, I expect things to take time.

The Lord shared with me that anything that I want in prayer will cost me something. It will cost my waiting and my patience. Prayer will always cost something because prayer is warfare. Prayer is circling the walls of Jericho for seven days, and the manifestation is when we shout to break the walls down. The world will see the walls come down and ask why, but they won't see you circling those walls in your prayer closet. But here is the thing, after the walls came down on Jericho, all the treasure that was in the city became holy. They came under the ownership of the Lord. And any man who claimed this was to be put to death. And the story goes that someone indeed took some of these items from Jericho and caused the whole camp to come under condemnation. To the point that in their next battle, they had to retreat because of the offensive that was caused. Don't go into your next battle claiming something that is God's. Your righteousness comes from Him. All your blessings come from Him. Have humility before the Lord and give Him glory and praise. But if you do not, then expecting a victory in prayer is foolishness. The lesson to learn is that in prayer, it may look like you are going in circles, but God is preparing to bring down walls. And out of that victory, give God the honor because if you don't, you will not win another victory till you give it to Him.

Esther and the King:

The story of Esther is an awesome story about how God can turn around what the enemy had planned for evil and instead give the victory to His people. To start off the story of Esther, I want to talk about how Esther got into a position to intercede for the Jews.

King Ahasuerus, who reigned from India to Ethiopia with 127 provinces, had dismissed his wife because she disgraced him. And the king was now looking for a new queen from the virgins of the land. So Esther was part of that group, and after receiving the favor of the king, she became the queen. Now, while Esther was a new queen, a man named Haman began to be promoted in the king's court. And in this promotion, many people had begun to give him honor by bowing in his presence, but when Mordecai, Esther's cousin, came to Haman, he did not bow. Haman took offense to this and decided that in retribution, he would sentence all the Jews of the land to death. He does this by telling the king that the Jews are enemies of the crown and promises to fill the king's coffers with wealth if the king would allow Haman to destroy the Jews. The king agrees with this decision and allows Haman to send out this order. Now, unknown to the king, Esther is a Jewish woman. So this order would also condemn her to death as well as the rest of the Jews. Mordecai then hears of this and tells Esther's eunuchs to tell her as well.

> **Mordecai told him all that had happened to him, and the exact amount of money that Haman had promised to pay to the king's treasuries for the destruction of the Jews. He also gave him a copy**

> *of the text of the edict which had been issued in Susa for their destruction, that he might show Esther and inform her, and to order her to go in to the king to implore his favor and to plead with him for her people.*
>
> *Esther 4:7-8*

So Esther ends up hearing this news about how there will soon be a genocide of her people by the order of the king through Haman. She now knows Mordecai is calling her to speak and plead with the king to stop this persecution that is going to happen to her people and to her.

> *"All the king's servants and the people of the king's provinces know that for any man or woman who comes to the king to the inner court who is not summoned, he has but one law, that he be put to death, unless the king holds out to him the golden scepter so that he may live. And I have not been summoned to come to the king for these thirty days."*
>
> *Esther 4:11*

Esther then tells Mordecai that the situation is not as easy as it appears. She reminds Mordecai that one of the rules of the kingdom is that no one is to go before the king unless they are called by him, and if they do, in fact, go before the king without being called, then they could be put to death. The only way to avoid being put to death is if the king favors you and lifts his golden scepter to you. So Esther would have to go before the king and risk being killed in order to try to petition the king to save her people.

> ***Then Esther told them to reply to Mordecai, "Go, assemble all the Jews who are found in Susa, and fast for me; do not eat or drink for three days, night or day. I and my maidens also will fast in the same way. And thus I will go in to the king, which is not according to the law; and if I perish, I perish."***
>
> ***Esther 4:15-16***

Esther bravely decides to go before the king without being called, and she asks all the Jews in Susa to fast to bless her attempt. Lastly, she says something amazing; she tells Mordecai that if she were to die, so be it. She looks death in the face and rises to the challenge in order to intercede for her people.

> *Now it came about on the third day that Esther put on her royal robes and stood in the inner court of the king's palace in front of the king's rooms, and the king was sitting on his royal throne in the throne room, opposite the entrance to the palace. When the king saw Esther the queen standing in the court, she obtained favor in his sight; and the king extended to Esther the golden scepter which was in his hand. So Esther came near and touched the top of the scepter.*

Esther 5:1-2

So Esther put on her royal robes and stood in the inner court of the king's palace. After the king had seen Esther, he granted her to be in his presence by extending his scepter toward the queen. This means that all Esther has to do now is tell the king of the plans that Haman has made. But instead of telling him right there, she tells the king that he is invited to a banquet, and Haman is invited as well. The king immediately summons Haman, and they go off to the banquet that Queen Esther had prepared. While the King is there, he asks Esther what she would desire, even up to half the kingdom. Now Esther doesn't tell the king that day but instead tells the king that if he comes to one more banquet tomorrow, then she will let the king know of her petition. So the king agrees to come tomorrow for another banquet. Now after the first banquet, Haman goes home, and while he is making his way there, he sees Mordecai. Now when he passes Mordecai, he expects to see him stand and be trembling before him because of what Haman plans to do to him. But instead of standing in respect and trembling before him, Mordecai sits and watches as Haman walks past him. This infuriates Haman, and when he comes home, he lets his friends and family know how he feels.

> *Haman also said, "Even Esther the queen let no one but me come with the king to the banquet which she had prepared; and tomorrow also I am invited by her with the king. Yet all of this does not satisfy me every time I see Mordecai the Jew sitting at the king's gate." Then Zeresh his wife and all his friends said to him, "Have a gallows fifty cubits high made and in the morning ask the king to have Mordecai hanged on*

it; then go joyfully with the king to the banquet." And the advice pleased Haman, so he had the gallows made.

Esther 5:12-14

When he had finished explaining to his wife and friends what his plight was, they suggested that he have a gallows of fifty cubits tall, seventy-five feet, to be made for the hanging of Mordecai. This, of course, was a great idea to Haman, so he had them made. After the night of the banquet, though, the king was having a hard time falling to sleep. So he asked that the record keeper come and read to him what had recently happened in his kingdom in order to pass the time. While having the records read to him, he found that it was Mordecai who had recently warned of an attempt on the king's life, and an assassination was avoided. The king asked if Mordecai was ever honored for what he did, and it turned out that nothing was done for him. So the king called his servant Haman and asked him what should be done for a man that the king wanted to honor. Haman, thinking that the king was desiring to honor him, told the king that the man should have royal robes placed on him, riding on a royal horse, and to be led by a noble prince who would proclaim through the streets of the city that this is what the king will do for those who he honors.

> **Then the king said to Haman, "Take quickly the robes and the horse as you have said, and do so for Mordecai the Jew, who is sitting at the king's gate; do not fall short in anything of all that you have said." So Haman took the robe and the horse, and arrayed Mordecai, and led him on horseback through the city square, and proclaimed before him, "Thus it shall be done to the man whom the king desires to honor."**
>
> **Esther 6:10-11**

So then the king told Haman to do all that he suggested to the man Mordecai, and that he should not stray from anything that was suggested. Then Haman led Mordecai through the streets of Susa, the capital, and honored him before all in the city. After this was done, Haman went to his house in shame, where he told his friends and family what happened, and then was taken by the eunuchs to the second banquet hosted by Esther. When everyone was at the banquet, Esther let the king know her petition.

> *Then Queen Esther replied, "If I have found favor in your sight, O king, and if it pleases the king, let my life be given me as my petition, and my people as my request; for we have been sold, I and my people, to be destroyed, to be killed and to be annihilated. Now if we had only been sold as slaves, men and women, I would have remained silent, for the trouble would not be commensurate with the annoyance to the king."*
>
> *Esther 7:3-4*

Esther begins to plead her case before the king and lets the king know what is happening to her people. She comes to the king in humility and lets the king know that if it were just for the purpose of slavery, she would not have bothered the king, but with the matter being about life and death, she had to come to him.

> *Then King Ahasuerus asked Queen Esther, "Who is he, and where is he, who would presume to do thus?" Esther said, "A foe and an enemy is this wicked Haman!" Then Haman became terrified before the king and queen.*
> *Esther 7:5-6*

The king then becomes very angry when he hears what has happened to his queen and her people. The king then goes off to his garden to calm down. While the king is away, Haman pleads for his life and petitions the queen that she would spare him. He pleads to the point where he had fallen on the couch that Esther was on. The king's anger then increased and desired to have Haman killed.

> **Then Harbonah, one of the eunuchs who were before the king said, "Behold indeed, the gallows standing at Haman's house fifty cubits high, which Haman made for Mordecai who spoke good on behalf of the king!" And the king said, "Hang him on it." So they hanged Haman on the gallows which he had prepared for Mordecai, and the king's anger subsided.**
>
> **Esther 7:9-10**

So Haman was hung on the very gallows that he had made for Mordecai. After this, the queen pleaded with the king that the Jewish people would be saved from the planned genocide. There was a problem though, and it had to do with a rule that was in the kingdom at the time. If a king made a decree, even the king himself could not undo it. That was the power of the king's seal, and Haman used this seal when he called for the Jews to be murdered. So the king decides to allow all the Jews in the land the ability to defend themselves and to destroy anyone who is attacking them. So when the massacre was supposed to happen, instead, there was a great victory for all the Jews in the kingdom because they destroyed all those who had hated them and wanted to kill them. This event was called Purim and is now a holiday that the Jewish people celebrate to this day! But there are some very interesting connections between Purim and what God does in a believer's life. First of all, we know that as believers, we are called the bride of Christ.

> *For this reason a man shall leave his father and mother and shall be joined to his wife, and the two shall become one flesh. This mystery is great; but I am speaking with reference to Christ and the church.*
>
> *Ephesians 5:31-32*

With that being said, we can see ourselves in the same position that Esther is in when she interceded for her people. We, as the bride, have a unique position with the King, not of an earthly kingdom, but the

King of all creation. And a lot of Christians have the same kind of attitude that Esther had in this story; they think that if they come before their husband, they may be "killed."

But the Bible tells us that the king had so much love and favor toward Esther that the king not only went to a banquet with the queen one day but also the next day after that! This busy king loved his wife so much that he didn't care if there were two banquets in a row. Not only did he come to her banquets, but he also loved her so much that he offered her up to half of the kingdom! That is some extreme favor! And I want us to recognize that we have that same kind of favor that we have with Jesus. He wants to give us everything! So we need to come boldly before the throne, just as Paul says.

> ***Therefore let us draw near with confidence to the throne of grace, so that we may receive mercy and find grace to help in time of need.***
>
> ***Hebrews 4:16***

The next thing that is symbolic of the relationship that we have with God is the kind of victory that Mordecai, Esther, and the Jews had. The same honor that Haman wanted Mordecai to give was given to

Mordecai by Haman himself. The same gallows that were made for Mordecai were used to hang Haman. All the enemies of the Jews that wanted to destroy them were destroyed themselves by the Jews. God wants to take every enemy in your life and flip the tables on them. Every scheme and plan is going to be reversed for your victory. We have become more than conquerors in Christ! And the last thing that is prophetic of the church is that the solution to stopping the genocide of the Jews was not to command it to stop, but rather it was about allowing the Jews to defend themselves. This is the same way with the church! We have not been taken out of the world, but we have been called to make war with the enemies of Christ.

> ***I also say to you that you are Peter, and upon this rock I will build My church; and the gates of Hades will not overpower it.***
>
> ***Matthew 16:18***

One of my favorite teachings ever is when Jesus tells Peter that the gates of Hades will not overpower the church. Now for a while, I didn't think much of this verse till someone let me know that by Jesus saying the gates of Hades, He was talking about offense, not defense. When you go to war, and you are conquering a stronghold, you attack the gates! We are to be conquering our enemies! Jesus left us to fight the good fight, and He equipped us with everything we need for the battle.

> ***Behold, I have given you authority to tread on serpents and scorpions, and over all the power of the enemy, and nothing will injure you.***
>
> ***Luke 10:19***

Now, the most important faith lesson that we can learn from Esther is that we are to be bold with our prayers and that we are to understand our position with Christ. We are His bride, and we are highly favored in His eyes. We have an immense privilege when it comes to prayers and petitions to God. If you can fully understand this revelation, it will strengthen your faith because the enemy will want you to think less of yourself so that you doubt your prayers. I promise that if you stick in there with your prayers, you will see a breakthrough because the Lord loves you and because you are His church, His bride!

Chapter 7

Learning From the Old Testament Part 2

Ruth and Boaz

The next story that I want to go over with you guys is that of Ruth and Boaz. Now this story is about a kinsman redeemer and a Gentile daughter-in-law. This is a great story to talk about how Jesus also is a type of kinsman redeemer, but that is beyond the scope of this chapter and book. I want to focus mostly on how we can learn about faith from this awesome woman of God! The story starts with the introduction of Naomi, an Israelite woman, and her two sons. Now these sons were living in the land of Moab when their father died, and they both took Moabite wives for themselves. But they both tragically died, and Naomi was left without sons and without a husband. She then tells both her daughters-in-law that she is leaving back to Israel and that they don't have to stay with her. They all were sad, and one of her daughters-in-law, Orpha, decided to go back to her father's house in Moab. But Ruth decided to stay with Naomi and wouldn't leave her side. They make their way back to the land of Judah and come into the city of Bethlehem, around the time of the barley harvest. Now while they are there, Ruth decides that it would be a good idea to go and pick up the grain that is left over after the reapers have chopped down the barley harvest. When she goes to find a field in which she can glean, she happens to come to the field of Boaz. Now Boaz was from the same family of Naomi's husband, so he is considered eligible for being a kinsman redeemer. The role of a kinsman redeemer is to preserve the inheritance of a family member by taking that person's widow and having a child with her. This way, that child will receive his father's inheritance and preserve his father's name in Israel. While Ruth is gleaning in the fields, Boaz comes to see the reapers who are working in his field and asks about Ruth. After learning that the woman gleaning his field is the woman that came back with Naomi, he decides to bless her.

> **Then Boaz said to Ruth, "Listen carefully, my daughter. Do not go to glean in another field; furthermore, do not go on from this one, but stay here with my maids. Let your eyes be on the field which they reap, and go after them.**

> *Indeed, I have commanded the servants not to touch you. When you are thirsty, go to the water jars and drink from what the servants draw."*
>
> *Ruth 2:8-9 NASB1995*

Boaz just gave her permission to gather after the reapers and made sure that the reapers won't bother her. This means that Ruth just got the ability to provide for Naomi and herself. This is an amazing thing to have in the ancient world, where, without a man, it was hard to provide for yourself as a woman. Ruth then asks Boaz why she has received such favor.

> *Then she fell on her face, bowing to the ground and said to him, "Why have I found favor in your sight that you should take notice of me, since I am a foreigner?" Boaz replied to her, "All that you have done for your mother-in-law after the death of your husband has been fully reported to me, and how you left your father and your mother and the land of your birth, and came to a people that you did not previously know.*
>
> *Ruth 2:10-11*

Boaz wanted to favor Ruth because of what she did for Naomi. Now this can be a lesson for us as well. When we love those people around us, God will see that and show us favor just as Boaz did with Ruth. And after Ruth worked for a little, Boaz told his servants that they were to bless Ruth even more!

> **When she rose to glean, Boaz commanded his servants, saying, "Let her glean even among the sheaves, and do not insult her. Also you shall purposely pull out for her some grain from the bundles and leave it that she may glean, and do not rebuke her."**
>
> **Ruth 2:15-16**

This is what God does for you! Sometimes he does things that you don't even know about because He loves you. He favors you in your work when you haven't even asked Him for anything. This is because He is a good Father. After Ruth gleaned the field for the day, she gathered an ephah of barley, which is roughly forty-eight pounds of barley. This is a huge amount of barley for a widow and her daughter-in-law. Now after Naomi hears about the favor that was shown to Ruth, she asks who was the man that had been so kind to Ruth. As soon as Naomi hears that it is the man Boaz, she recognizes that this man qualifies to be a kinsman redeemer. So Naomi tells Ruth what to do so that they will be redeemed in Israel.

> ***Then Naomi her mother-in-law said to her, "My daughter, shall I not seek security for you, that it may be well with you? Now is not Boaz our kinsman, with whose maids you were? Behold, he winnows barley at the threshing floor tonight. Wash yourself therefore, and anoint yourself and put on your best clothes, and go down to the threshing floor; but do not make yourself known to the man until he has finished eating and drinking. It shall be when he lies down, that you shall notice the place where he lies, and you shall go and uncover his feet and lie down; then he will tell you what you shall do." She said to her, "All that you say I will do."***
>
> ***Ruth 3:1-5***

So after Naomi tells Ruth what to do, Ruth goes to Boaz at the threshing floor. Once she gets there, Boaz recognizes his role as the kinsman redeemer for

Ruth. He tells Ruth that there is another relative that is closer in relation and is more qualified to redeem her. If he does not redeem Ruth, then Boaz will. So Boaz goes off to the city to find this man who is the other potential redeemer. After they talk for a while, Boaz ends up redeeming Ruth, and he takes her as his wife. The son of Ruth and Boaz ends up being Obed, who is the father of Jesse. Jesse then becomes the father of David, the king of Israel. So think about the legacy that Ruth and Boaz had as part of the kingly lineage of Israel. But let's go over what Ruth can teach us about faith. Now there isn't any specific instance where Ruth was walking in faith before God, but there are some important lessons in obedience and love. Now the first thing to learn is how loving others can lead to our favor.

> *In that day you will ask in My name, and I do not say to you that I will request of the Father on your behalf; for the Father Himself loves you, because you have loved Me and have believed that I came forth from the Father.*
>
> *John 16:26-27*

This is the connection between love and answered prayer. It is our love of Jesus that causes the Father to love us. This then means that we can speak directly to the Father to have our requests answered. But how do we love Jesus? Do we praise Him? Do we spend time reading about Him?

> ***"If you love Me, you will keep My commandments.***
>
> ***John 14:15***

So we know that if we love Jesus, we will keep His commandments. Yes, praising Him and reading His Word will increase our relationship with Him, but the foundation of that relationship will always be obedience. Now this shouldn't ever be a reluctant obedience because if we are followers of Christ, we agree that His ways are good. So it is an obedience that is about fighting off temptation and our fleshly desires. And this is how Ruth is a picture of faith because she had both love and obedience, which lead to favor. Ruth had love when she followed Naomi back to Judah, and she had obedience when she did as Naomi commanded when it came to Boaz. If Ruth had not listened to Naomi, she would have never been redeemed by Boaz, and she would have never had the honor to be part of the lineage of Jesus. And in the same way, we receive favor and have our prayers answered when we love Jesus by obeying

Him. This is part of faith, to have the favor in your life where everything you pray about is answered. So the lesson that we can learn from Ruth is that if we want God to move in favor in our lives, we need to love Jesus. And the foundation of loving Jesus is following His commands. And lastly, before Ruth was taken as the wife of Boaz, she washed herself and put on clean clothes. When Jesus comes to take us as His bride, we, too, will be cleaned and clothed with new white robes. Let the Lord discipline you so that you will be clean with the blood of Jesus and clothed with righteousness.

Noah and His Ark:

The next story that I want to talk about is the story of Noah and his ark. So Noah has an amazing story of faith that has to do with waiting on the Lord on His timing that I want to share with you guys. So let's check out the story of Noah!

> *The Lord said, "I will blot out man whom I have created from the face of the land, from man to animals to creeping things and to birds of the sky; for I am sorry that I have made them." But Noah found favor in the eyes of the Lord. These are the records of the*

> *generations of Noah. Noah was a righteous man, blameless in his time; Noah walked with God.*
>
> *Genesis 6:7-9*

The story on Noah starts out with God deciding to destroy mankind because they had become corrupt in their ways and in their flesh. But the Lord looked on Noah with favor and had planned to use him to repopulate the earth with humanity. The reason for this is that Noah was a righteous man and blameless in his time. The important thing to see is that Noah was chosen by God to repopulate the earth because Noah walked with God in a relationship. So the Lord tells Noah what He is going to do and lets Noah know what he should do to survive the judgment.

> *Then God said to Noah, "The end of all flesh has come before Me; for the earth is filled with violence because of them; and behold, I am about to destroy them with the earth. Make for yourself an ark of gopher wood; you shall make the ark with rooms, and shall cover it inside and out with pitch.*
>
> *Genesis 6:13-14*

Now that Noah has the command from the Lord, he goes off and builds himself a giant ark. This ark needs to be big enough to fill all the types of animals on the earth. Before the flood waters come, all the animals that are needed are brought into the ark, and Noah and his family get onto the ark. Then when the flood waters come, only those on the ark are able to survive the rising waters. In fact, the waters rise so high that the mountains were covered.

> *Also the fountains of the deep and the floodgates of the sky were closed, and the rain from the sky was restrained; and the water receded steadily from the earth, and at the end of one hundred and fifty days the water decreased. In the seventh month, on the seventeenth day of the month, the ark rested upon the mountains of Ararat. The water decreased steadily until the tenth month; in the tenth month, on the first day of the month, the tops of the mountains became visible.*
>
> ***Genesis 8:2-5***

And it was a long time till the waters had come down from covering those mountains. Could you imagine being Noah as he longed and waited to go back onto dry ground again? Now the ark had rested on the mountain, and the tops of all the mountains were starting to be revealed, but the Lord hadn't given Noah the command to leave yet.

> *Then he sent out a dove from him, to see if the water was abated from the face of the land; but the dove found no resting place for the sole of her foot, so she returned to him into the ark, for the water was on the surface of all the earth. Then he put out his hand and took her, and brought her into the ark to himself. So he waited yet another seven days; and again he sent out the dove from the ark. The dove came to him toward evening, and behold, in her beak was a freshly picked olive leaf. So Noah knew that the water was abated from the earth.*
>
> ***Genesis 8:8-11***

Noah even had a system of using a dove to tell if the land had dried up. And after he received that olive leaf, believe he was really excited to leave the ark and go out onto land again. But the Lord never told him to leave, so he had to wait in the ark.

> ***Now it came about in the six hundred and first year, in the first month, on the first of the month, the water was dried up from the earth. Then Noah removed the covering of the ark, and looked, and behold, the surface of the ground was dried up. In the second month, on the twenty-seventh day of the month, the earth was dry. Then God spoke to Noah, saying, "Go out of the ark, you and your wife and your sons and your sons' wives with you.***
>
> ***Genesis 8:13-16***

Finally, after it had been multiple months of waiting, Noah was released to go onto the land again. Now you might have thought that Noah could have gone at least on top of the mountain and the waters had receded. Or maybe he could have gone out when he saw that the olive branch was brought in by the dove. Or he could have even gone out when he looked out of the covering to see with his very own eyes that the earth was dry! But Noah waited till the Lord gave him the command to leave, even when with his own eyes and understanding, he could have left. This is the kind of faith that we need to have as believers in Christ. We need to stay still and not move until the Lord tells us. Noah was a man of patience and faith. He didn't rely on his own understanding but was patient in waiting on the Lord. Timing is everything with God. He knows how the world operates and has a higher perspective on life. If you wait and trust in Him, you will do well.

> ***Throughout all their journeys whenever the cloud was taken up from over the tabernacle, the sons of Israel would set out; but if the cloud was not taken up, then they did not set out until the day when it was taken up.***
>
> ***Exodus 40:36-37***

All of Israel had to have this kind of patience and trust when they were in the desert on their way to the promised land. They wouldn't move unless the Lord moved.

> ***It shall be, when you hear the sound of marching in the tops of the balsam trees, then you shall act promptly, for***

> **then the Lord will have gone out before you to strike the army of the Philistines."**

2 Samuel 5:24

David had to wait patiently with his army as the Philistines crossed right in front of him.

He had to trust and rely on the Lord that His promise of victory was true. But he also had to follow the command of the Lord. I wonder what would have happened if David went by his own understanding and not the Lord's? Would he have died in that battle, or would his impatience have spelled the end of David's kingdom because he lost a battle with the Philistines? The timing of the Lord is important, and though it may seem like God is not moving or He has abandoned you, it is not the case.

> **The Lord is not slow about His promise, as some count slowness, but is patient toward you, not wishing for any to perish but for all to come to repentance.**

2 Peter 3:9

So to recap the lesson of Noah, it is important to wait on God's timing. His ways are higher than our ways, and His perspective is higher than our perspective. Even when it seems like the time to move, be like Noah and wait in the ark that the Lord has given you.

Daniel and Gabriel

The next story that I want to talk about is the story of Daniel. Now Daniel is one of my favorite Bible characters because the Lord had made him wise and powerful in the kingdom of Babylon. Now Daniel was blessed to come into this position based on his heritage as a noble of Israel, but it was also because Daniel was a strong believer and follower of the Lord. The stories that I want to go over with you are the story of Daniel and the lions' den, and the story of Daniel and the twenty-one-day fast. I think these are some super important stories about understanding faith and prayer. So let's check them out.

> ***Then this Daniel began distinguishing himself among the commissioners and satraps because he possessed an extraordinary spirit, and the king planned to appoint him over the entire kingdom. Then the commissioners and satraps began trying to find a ground of accusation against Daniel in regard to government affairs; but they could***

> ***find no ground of accusation or evidence of corruption, inasmuch as he was faithful, and no negligence or corruption was to be found in him.***
>
> ***Daniel 6:3-4***

The beginning of the story of Daniel and the lions' den starts out with Daniel succeeding and prospering in his position as commissioner. Now this caused the other commissioners and satraps to conspire to destroy Daniel. This may have been because he wasn't allowing them to be corrupt or maybe they were jealous of his success. Either way, they went to gather evidence of any corruption or negligence and couldn't find anything. Daniel was found to be innocent even in the eyes of those who hated him. So the evil men decided to come up with a scheme to destroy Daniel by the king's hand. They decided that if they were ever going to get Daniel, they would have to use his integrity against him. And they knew that the only thing stronger than Daniel's loyalty to the king was his loyalty to God.

> ***All the commissioners of the kingdom, the prefects and the satraps, the high officials and the governors have consulted together that the king should***

> *establish a statute and enforce an injunction that anyone who makes a petition to any god or man besides you, O king, for thirty days, shall be cast into the lions' den.*

Daniel 6:7

All the commissioners and satraps that desired to destroy Daniel came to the king with a proposal. They suggested that as a way to honor the king, the king should make a statue that if anyone were to petition any god or man beside the king for thirty days, then they are to be fed to the lions. Now this appealed to the king's pride, so he implemented this statute. The interesting thing to note here is that when these commissioners and satraps came to the king, they told him that all the commissioners and satraps were in agreement with this statute. So the men lied to him because we know that Daniel would never agree to such a proposal. This may have been the reason why he agreed to do it, assuming he knew Daniel's faithfulness to God.

> *Now when Daniel knew that the document was signed, he entered his house (now in his roof chamber he had windows open toward Jerusalem); and he*

> ***continued kneeling on his knees three times a day, praying and giving thanks before his God, as he had been doing previously. Then these men came by agreement and found Daniel making petition and supplication before his God.***
>
> ***Daniel 6:10-11***

This is probably one of the most impressive examples of faith in the Bible. It is on par with how the early church fathers faced the oppressive political system of Rome and how there are Christians who face persecution around the world today. Daniel knew what would become of him if he continued to pray and thank God, but yet he still worshiped the Lord. He didn't care that he was a high-ranking official in the government of Babylon. He didn't care that he had power and wealth that would have made the everyday man jealous. All he cared about was his relationship with God. This is because Daniel not only had a relationship with God, but he also had an understanding that without God, he wouldn't have been in that place of privilege at all. These verses also give us some insight into the spiritual life of Daniel. He was so dedicated to God that he would come to the Lord three times a day! That is awesome! We should take a note out of Daniel's book and start praying like this. After these men came and found Daniel praying, they came before the king to accuse Daniel. Now after hearing this, the king was distraught. One, because he assumed all the commissioners were on board with the statute, and also because Daniel was the best man in his government. If the king were to lose Daniel, he would be losing an important part of his rule. So the king spent all day trying to come up with ways in which he could save Daniel. Yet he was unable to save Daniel because of a rule that we talked about earlier with the story of Esther.

> ***Then these men came by agreement to the king and said to the king, "Recognize, O king, that it is a law of the Medes and Persians that no injunction or statute which the king establishes may be changed."***
>
> ***Daniel 6:15***

There was no way that the king could save Daniel. It was impossible for him to revoke the command that he had given. The king then calls for Daniel to be brought to the lions' den and to be shut up in it for the night. Afterward, the king leaves and fasts for Daniel's life to be saved. This can show us the heart of the king in this situation. He truly desired to save Daniel, probably because Daniel was such a great servant of his. With all the power that the king had, it wasn't enough to save Daniel. But the king was wise enough to fast and petition God so that Daniel might be saved. This is a lesson that we can learn from the king, that even when we have exhausted all of the worldly options for salvation, God is still there to save. In the morning, the king rushes to the lions' den and calls out to Daniel. That is when Daniel responds.

> *My God sent His angel and shut the lions' mouths and they have not harmed me, inasmuch as I was found innocent before Him; and also toward you, O king, I have committed no crime."*
>
> *Daniel 6:22*

The Lord then rescues Daniel from the lions' den, and the king returns Daniel to his place as commissioner. He also takes all the people that accused Daniel and throws them into the same lions' den that was meant for Daniel. This is similar, though, to our situation. It is true that Daniel was guilty for the crime that he was accused of. But it was by the providence of God that the mouths of the lions were shut. And in the same way we are guilty of our sins, yet the

Lord shuts the mouth of hell and throws down our accusers into that same pit. But let's talk about all the things we can learn from Daniel. Why did God save him? It wasn't an act of faith that caused him to be saved. It wasn't him facing down Goliath. He didn't boldly walk through Pharaoh's courts. But instead, the faith wasn't doing what God asked, but, instead, showing loyalty to God in the face of persecution. And this is why he was saved. Not because of faith in action, but in his faith as a relationship. Daniel was a man that received special favor and privileges all his life because of his relationship with the Lord. You see, part of faith is about building a relationship where you get special treatment. God is not so different to not bless those who are closest to Him. God is not partial in judgment, but he is partial in favor and blessing. So the trick to having a life full of blessing and favor is to be close to the one who gives all good things. And how do we do that? We take time out of our day to petition, thank, and praise Him. We spend time in His Word. He is a real person. As soon as you stop seeing God as far beyond you and start seeing Him as a personable being that loves you, then you can start your relationship with God. Let's go on to the next story about Daniel and the angel Gabriel. Now this story starts out with Daniel receiving a dream from the Lord. Daniel was known for being able to discern dreams, but when he got this dream from the Lord, he sought to get a deeper understanding of it.

> *In those days, I, Daniel, had been mourning for three entire weeks. I did not eat any tasty food, nor did meat or wine enter my mouth, nor did I use any ointment at all until the entire three weeks were completed.*
>
> *Daniel 10:2-3*

So Daniel fasted for twenty-one days, and then the angel Gabriel appeared to him to explain the vision. But I don't want to talk about the vision, though it is an important subject, I want to talk about a small detail that Gabriel gave Daniel.

> *Then he said to me, "Do not be afraid, Daniel, for from the first day that you set your heart on understanding this and on humbling yourself before your God, your words were heard, and I have come in response to your words. But the prince of the kingdom of Persia was withstanding me for twenty-one days; then behold, Michael, one of the*

chief princes, came to help me, for I had been left there with the kings of Persia.

Daniel 10:12-13

These have always been some super interesting verses to me because I feel that they show us a sneak peek into the spiritual realm. Here is what Gabriel told Daniel. That on the first day of fasting and praying, Gabriel was sent to bring Daniel the message. And if it wasn't for this entity called "the prince of Persia," Gabriel would have gotten to Daniel on the first day. This is super encouraging for us as believers because it is the same way for us. God wants us to have our answer as soon as we ask. But sometimes the enemy is holding back your breakthrough. This verse should inspire any Christian to keep on praying even when you have been waiting for a long time. Imagine if Daniel had quit at twenty days of fasting and never got that message from Gabriel. When we face times of prayer, we have to know that there is another side to what you are doing. Even though you can't see it, there is a battle going on for your request. So take courage in the fight and don't give up. Don't let delay take away your victory. Oftentimes, we can set up dates and times in our minds about when our prayers should be answered. But the most important thing to set your eyes on is Jesus and His faithfulness.

Jesus wouldn't have told you to pray if it didn't work. Your prayers are working even though you can't see it. This is the lesson that we can learn from Daniel. Prayer is warfare, and every prayer that we make will cost us something. It will cost an angel fighting the enemies of God, and it will cost your time and diligence. Stand strong in the Lord and take courage.

> ***Have I not commanded you? Be strong and courageous! Do not tremble or be dismayed, for the Lord your God is with you wherever you go."***
>
> ***Joshua 1:9***

Gideon and the Three Hundred

The last story that we are going to cover from the Old Testament is the story of Gideon and the three hundred. I think this is an important story to cover because it can teach us a lot about faith and how God works in our lives. The story starts with the nation of Midian oppressing the Israelites for seven years. This was because the Israelites had fallen into idolatry and lost the protection of God. God was about to raise up a deliverer for the people of Israel. And the person that God had chosen for this role was

Gideon the son of Joash. So the Lord sent an angel to let Gideon know what he was to do.

> ***Then the angel of the Lord came and sat under the oak that was in Ophrah, which belonged to Joash the Abiezrite as his son Gideon was beating out wheat in the wine press in order to save it from the Midianites. The angel of the Lord appeared to him and said to him, "The Lord is with you, O valiant warrior."***
>
> ***Judges 6:11-12***

The first thing that this angel tells Gideon is that he is a valiant warrior. I would like to contrast this by the fact that Gideon was hiding in a winepress at the time. The Lord decides to tell Gideon who he is rather than let Gideon decide for himself. The Lord often does this for us as well. He can fundamentally change us just by saying a word. This is the power of God because through words, He spoke the universe into existence.

> ***But the Lord said to him, "Surely I will be with you, and you shall defeat Midian as one man." So Gideon said***

> *to Him, "If now I have found favor in Your sight, then show me a sign that it is You who speak with me.*

Judges 6:16-17

Now Gideon has some unbelief in him and wanted to know whether he was hearing from God or not. So he asks the Lord for a sign that he may confirm the calling that was spoken over him. Gideon decides that before this man leaves him, he wants to bring him an offering. He then goes and brings back all the food for the offering. The angel tells Gideon to place the offering on a rock to see the sign.

> *Then the angel of the Lord put out the end of the staff that was in his hand and touched the meat and the unleavened bread; and fire sprang up from the rock and consumed the meat and the unleavened bread. Then the angel of the Lord vanished from his sight.*

Judges 6:21

Gideon gets the sign he was looking for and realizes that the man he was speaking with was, in fact, an angel. Later that same day, Gideon again hears from the Lord as to what he must do.

> *Now on the same night the Lord said to him, "Take your father's bull and a second bull seven years old, and pull down the altar of Baal which belongs to your father, and cut down the Asherah that is beside it; and build an altar to the Lord your God on the top of this stronghold in an orderly manner, and take a second bull and offer a burnt offering with the wood of the Asherah which you shall cut down." Then Gideon took ten men of his servants and did as the Lord had spoken to him; and because he was too afraid of his father's household and the men of the city to do it by day, he did it by night.*
>
> **Judges 6:25-27**

Now it is completely commendable that Gideon did something so brave as to tear down the altar of Baal and the Asherah that was beside it as the people held these idols with reverence. But he also did it in the night. This is there that we will continue to see in Gideon. That though he has faith and is obedient, he struggles with fear. When the men of the city wake to find that the altar of their god has been destroyed and their Asherah has become firewood on another altar, they are infuriated. They do some investigating and learn that it was Gideon who did this thing, so they call for his death. But the father of Gideon intercedes and says that if Baal is being disgraced, then let Baal bring the judgment. Basically, he is putting Baal to the test. Of course, nothing happens to Gideon, so he was unharmed for tearing down their altar. Then Gideon does another very bold thing.

> ***So the Spirit of the Lord came upon Gideon; and he blew a trumpet, and the Abiezrites were called together to follow him. He sent messengers throughout Manasseh, and they also were called together to follow him; and he sent messengers to Asher, Zebulun, and Naphtali, and they came up to meet them.***
>
> ***Judges 6:34-35***

When the Spirit of the Lord came upon Gideon, he rose up in boldness and blew a trumpet of war. He sent out messengers and called the people of Israel to rise up against Midian. Yet even in this boldness, there was some doubt. What is interesting to note here is that the boldness that Gideon had came from the Spirit of God. Though he was saved from judgment when he had destroyed the altars, and though he saw an angel of the Lord, he was still in unbelief. So he asked the Lord for a sign to confirm that he should lead Israel.

> ***Then Gideon said to God, "If You will deliver Israel through me, as You have spoken, behold, I will put a fleece of wool on the threshing floor. If there is dew on the fleece only, and it is dry on all the ground, then I will know that You will deliver Israel through me, as You have spoken."***
>
> ***Judges 6:36-37***

This sign and story of this sign is a classic Bible tale. What happened is that Gideon asks for the sign of dew on the fleece, and after he gets the sign, he asks for the opposite to happen. So the Lord works with Gideon's unbelief and provides him another sign. This is showing us an underlying issue with Gideon and with unbelief. When it comes to unbelief, it doesn't matter if you get a sign from God. Because unbelief is a worldview that reads everything in light of disbelief. Every sign and word from God that you receive will be twisted to unbelief. Even though an angel appeared to Gideon, he couldn't believe that he would be chosen to deliver the Israelites. Even though he had the sign of the fleece, he needed another because he "just had to be sure." After receiving his two signs, Gideon gathered up the people to go to war. But there was a problem.

> ***The Lord said to Gideon, "The people who are with you are too many for Me to give Midian into their hands, for Israel would become boastful, saying, 'My own power has delivered me.'***
>
> ***Judges 7:2***

There were so many people that had shown up to fight Midian that if they were to win, it would look like they did it. So God had to shrink the army of Israel. This is an interesting look into the perspective of God in this situation. God wasn't concerned with winning the battle because he knew he would. God was interested in the heart of the people, whether or not they would follow Him or give into pride. This often can happen in our lives as well. Sometimes the Lord needs to shrink you to show you how big He is. If He didn't shrink you, then when you get your deliverance, you might think it came by your own hand and not His. Remember this, that just because it feels like God is shrinking you, it doesn't mean He won't give you the victory. It just means He is gonna let you know how it happened. With that being said, the Lord needed to shrink the army of Israel to glorify Himself. He tells Gideon to allow anyone who is afraid to go home. This caused twenty-two thousand men to flee the fight, leaving only ten thousand left. Yet, for God, this was still too much. So He gave Midian the order to distinguish the men by how they drank water.

> ***The Lord said to Gideon, "I will deliver you with the 300 men who lapped and will give the Midianites into your hands; so let all the other people go, each man to his home."***

Judges 7:7

The Lord had whittled down the army of Israel to only three hundred men from thirty-two thousand. That is a huge loss in numbers, but it didn't matter to the Lord. So the army of the Lord was three hundred men, and the rest went back to their homes. The Lord then tells Gideon to go by himself down to the camp of the Midianites to see what the Lord has done for Israel.

> *Now the same night it came about that the Lord said to him, "Arise, go down against the camp, for I have given it into your hands. But if you are afraid to go down, go with Purah your servant down to the camp, and you will hear what they say; and afterward your hands will be strengthened that you may go down against the camp." So he went with Purah his servant down to the outposts of the army that was in the camp.*
>
> *Judges 7:9-11*

But the Lord also lets Gideon know that if he is afraid, he can take his servant Purah with him. Gideon, of course, takes along Purah to spy out the camp of the enemy, staying consistent to the track record of fear and unbelief that he has. And when they get down to the camp, they overhear a conversation between two men about a dream one of them had.

> *When Gideon came, behold, a man was relating a dream to his friend. And he said, "Behold, I had a dream; a loaf of barley bread was tumbling into the camp of Midian, and it came to the tent and struck it so that it fell, and turned it upside down so that the tent lay flat." His friend replied, "This is nothing less than the sword of Gideon the son of Joash, a man of Israel; God has given Midian and all the camp into his hand."*
>
> *Judges 7:13-14*

The Lord took Gideon down to the enemy camp to show him how the battle was already won. The hearts of the people had been supernaturally given over to fear by the hand of the Lord. When Gideon heard this, he immediately started to worship the Lord. This is a commendable display of reverence from Gideon that is important. Gideon was worshiping because he knew that the Lord had given him the battle. We can also worship in faith just like Gideon did. When the Lord lets you see how you are going to win, worship Him in that moment. Gideon then goes up and lets the army know what the plan is. All the men were to have trumpets and pitchers with lit torches inside. Then they were to surround the camp of the enemy, and at the same time, they all blew their trumpets and broke the pitchers to reveal the torches.

> ***When the three companies blew the trumpets and broke the pitchers, they held the torches in their left hands and the trumpets in their right hands for blowing, and cried, "A sword for the Lord and for Gideon!" Each stood in his place around the camp; and all the army ran, crying out as they fled. When they blew 300 trumpets, the Lord set the sword of one against another even throughout the whole army; and the army fled as far as Beth-shittah toward Zererah, as far as the edge of Abel-meholah, by Tabbath.***
>
> ***Judges 7:20-22***

Now this caused the whole army of the Midianites to flee in terror and started in fighting amongst the army. The fog of war and terror in the camp brought about the defeat of the Midianites. This was the work of the Lord. After they fled, Gideon called the tribes of Asher, Naphtali, Manasseh, and Ephraim. They chased down all the armies of Midian and killed one hundred and twenty thousand men. Gideon then took his three hundred men and chased down the remaining army of the Midianites.

> ***Then Gideon and the 300 men who were with him came to the Jordan and crossed over, weary yet pursuing. Now Zebah and Zalmunna were in Karkor, and their armies with them, about 15,000 men, all who were left of the entire army of the sons of the east; for the fallen were 120,000 swordsmen. Gideon went up by the way of those who lived in tents on the east of Nobah and Jogbehah, and attacked the camp when the camp was unsuspecting.***
>
> ***Judges 8:4, 10-11***

Gideon was chasing down the kings of Midian with only his three hundred men. You can see that his faith and trust in God was increasing because, previously, he wouldn't have been brave enough to do this before. And we can see this because on the way to defeat the remaining army, he comes to two cities. And in those two cities, he asks them for food and supplies. But both of them refused because they do not believe Gideon will defeat the army. So Gideon made vows to punish both cities once he captured the kings. Gideon was riding the wave of faith and became bold enough to make those vows. And he paid both of them when he accomplished what he said he would do. After this great victory over the Midianites, the men of Israel desired Gideon to become king over all of Israel.

> *Then the men of Israel said to Gideon, "Rule over us, both you and your son, also your son's son, for you have delivered us from the hand of Midian." But Gideon said to them, "I will not rule over you, nor shall my son rule over you; the Lord shall rule over you." Yet Gideon said to them, "I would request of you, that each of you give me an earring from his spoil." (For they had gold earrings, because they were Ishmaelites.)*
>
> *Judges 8:22-24 NASB1995*

But Gideon decided to wisely leave the ruling of Israel to the Lord. This is a great show of humility because he could have just taken the throne and ruled all of Israel. He instead just asked for earrings of gold. Gideon then took the gold and made it into a golden ephod.

> **Gideon made it into an ephod, and placed it in his city, Ophrah, and all Israel played the harlot with it there, so that it became a snare to Gideon and his household.**
>
> **Judges 8:27**

Gideon yet again goes against the very thing that he had just previously done. He received a sign from an angel and followed the command of the Lord to tear down the altar of Baal, but he did it at night because he was afraid. He blew the horn to summon all the armies of Israel yet had to ask for a sign to see if he was really supposed to lead them. He was told to go to the camp of the enemy but brought his servant along because he was afraid. He honors God by not becoming king, then he builds an idol that all Israel worships. The story of Gideon is that he was a double-minded man. He had faith, yet he was afraid at the same time. He honored God, yet he dishonored God. We need to learn from Gideon's mistakes. We need to be able to take what the Lord says to us and follow through with it. No, you don't need another sign from him. Don't undercut God's plan with your disbelief. The goal of this book is to get you from a Gideon to a David. No longer will you be in disbelief, but you will walk in confidence with the Lord. Gideon asked for many signs. David didn't ask for any when he slew Goliath.

A Review of the Lessons:

Before we end this chapter, I want to go over all the lessons that we learned from all these Old Testament Bible characters. We learned from David that we should remember that we are in covenant with the Lord and that we should stand on this covenant. We also learned that, like David, God will put us through situations that will prepare us for our giants. Just like David faced the lion and the bear before he faced Goliath, we learned that instead of taking up the armor of Saul, David walked out to face Goliath in his shepherd clothes. He didn't need any more equipment than what the Lord had already given him. And lastly, we learned that we need to take our battles from the physical into the spiritual. As a physical battle, Goliath should have won, but it was never a physical battle. David took it to a spiritual level when he came only in the name of the Lord. Goliath came with his size, armor, and weapons, but David came with the name of the Lord.

When we studied Moses, the first thing we learned is that sometimes when God gives us a mission, we doubt ourselves. But this doubt will be the reason for our failure if we believe it. God will never give you a mission that you cannot fulfill. We learned that sometimes when we are in a spiritual battle for our breakthrough, we need to keep asking and praying. Pharaoh would have never let the people go unless it was under compulsion from the Lord. Let God put pressure on your spiritual battles because that pressure is going to lead to breakthroughs. We learned that the denying of your prayer will only make it better. At first, Moses only asked for three days in the desert to worship, but in the end, it turned into a permanent exodus, and they plundered Egypt on their way out. God is going to make it worse for the enemy the longer he resists you. Another lesson that we learned from Moses is sometimes God will take the staff in our hand and make it into a serpent. Don't run away from the tools that God has given you. And the last thing that we learned from Moses is that God is the one who tells us who we are and who we aren't. When God tells you that you are brave, that is what you are. Don't let the world or even your own idea of

yourself dictate who you are. If the Lord created the worlds by His words, then when He speaks over you, there is a power that will change you.

We learned from Joshua that sometimes the Lord will work in mysterious ways when He wants to break down some walls. We learned that just like Rahab, we have a covenant of protection, and we also will become part of the family of God. We learned from Rahab that true faith is hearing, believing, and acting on that word that you received. We learned that the fall of Jericho is symbolic of our prayer lives. Though it looks like we are going around in circles, we can trust in the Lord that He will bring those walls down.

When going over the story of Esther, we learned about using our relationship with the king to intercede for people. We learned that we need to recognize our relationship with the king, so that we are not afraid to come to Him. We also learned that just as the Jews were given the power to defend themselves, we, too, have been given power to prevail against the gates of hell. We learned from Ruth that love and obedience would lead to favor in our lives. We also learned that it is our relationship with Christ that gives us the privilege of answered prayers, and that to obey Christ is to love Him. We learned from Noah that patience and waiting on the Lord is of the utmost importance. We saw how he had multiple opportunities to leave the ark, but he waited on the Lord to tell him when to leave. Waiting on the Lord and His timing is part of a mature faith.

Daniel taught us that a relationship with God is how we walk in favor and divine protection. This type of relationship is consistent and doesn't waver in the face of persecution. We learned that part of prayer is spiritual warfare. Delay in prayer may be caused by the battle that is going on in the heavenly realms. We need to remember this when we are thinking about giving up. Don't give up! God hears you. He wants to answer you, but He needs you to stand and fight for your prayer. When we read about Gideon, we saw how he was double-minded. We learned that if we want to walk in true faith, we should take the word of the Lord and believe it. You don't need confirmation every step of the way. Trust in the Lord and follow Him with all your heart. Now that we are done with these Old Testament stories, in the next chapter, we will be covering what Jesus has to teach us about faith.

Chapter 8

Lessons from Jesus

This chapter will be focused on the teaching of Jesus and, more specifically, what He taught about faith. Now we all know that Jesus had some powerful things to say about faith, the most classic being that with faith, we are able to move mountains. And we will be going over this passage in this chapter, but I want to share with you guys how I will be breaking down other passages. A while back, when I was reading the Gospels, the Lord showed me something about Jesus. Every time He mentioned faith, it was an opportunity for us to learn about what faith really is. Now I am not talking about when Jesus is explicitly teaching on faith, but rather every event when He either commended someone's faith or marveled at their lack of faith. We can do a type of contextual reengineering to learn something about faith. This was, in fact, the main reason for writing this book because I believed the Lord had put this on my heart to write about this study. With that being said, we have already covered one of the lessons about faith from Jesus in chapter five. The other lessons of faith will follow the same formula. Let's get started!

Jesus and the Centurion:

The first passage that I want to go over with you is the story of the centurion and his great faith. I think that this is a super important aspect of faith, and it is actually part of the foundation for building a really powerful faith. I chose this as the first part of Jesus's teachings because every other teaching that we will go over needs this understanding first. So let's break down the passage.

> ***Now Jesus started on His way with them; and when He was not far from the house, the centurion sent friends, saying to Him, "Lord, do not trouble Yourself further, for I am not worthy for You to come under my roof; for this reason I did not even consider myself worthy to come to You, but just say the word, and my servant will be healed. For I also am a man placed under authority, with soldiers under me; and I say to this one, 'Go!' and he goes, and to another, 'Come!' and he comes, and to my slave, 'Do this!' and he does it."***

Now when Jesus heard this, He marveled at him, and turned and said to the crowd that was following Him, "I say to you, not even in Israel have I found such great faith."

Luke 7:6-9

The first thing that I noticed about this verse is that the centurion said that Jesus was a man under authority. He said by telling Jesus that he was a man placed under authority also. By saying this, the centurion was recognizing Jesus's authority. And the centurion also recognized that Jesus was under the authority of God, the Father. Then the centurion states that he has soldiers under him, and that all he needs to do is give a command, and they will follow it. By saying this, he is implying that Jesus has the ability to speak to that which is under Him, and it will obey. So the centurion is stating that not only is Jesus under the authority of God, but also Jesus is over reality to the point where if He just spoke a word, the servant would be healed.

Now when Jesus heard this faith, the Scripture says that He marveled. I think it would be a wise thing to look at what Jesus marveled at. If we want to have faith like a centurion, we need to recognize who Jesus really is. He is the Son of God, and He is placed under the authority of the Father. And all things have been put underneath Him. The other thing to know is that the centurion knew that authority came from putting yourself under authority. The centurion saw that Jesus had authority because He was under the authority of God. From this, we learn that we also can have authority by putting ourselves under the authority of Christ. To the extent that we put ourselves under Christ and His teachings is the extent that we will wield His authority.

> *For He has put all things in subjection under His feet. But when He says, "All things are put in subjection," it is evident that He is excepted who put all things in subjection to Him.*
>
> *1 Corinthians 15:27*

Now I say that this is the foundation of a good faith because if we can't believe that God is who He says He is, then we can never trust Him. You have to let God be as big as He truly is. If we shrink Him down in our minds, then we won't call on Him for help, and we won't call on Him for guidance. The Father is above all things, and He has put all things under Jesus. That means that you have a brother, King, and High Priest who is over all power and authority. He can do anything and everything He wants, but if you don't allow Him to be there for you, then you will never see Him as He really is. That is why the centurion had such great faith because he saw Jesus as a man under authority and as a man that had great authority. This is the first step in building great faith.

> ***And Jesus said to the centurion, "Go; it shall be done for you as you have believed." And the servant was healed that very moment.***
>
> ***Matthew 8:13***

The last thing that we learn from this passage is that Jesus tells the centurion that it shall be done for him as he has believed. What is interesting about this is Jesus was going to help the centurion by going to his house, but the centurion believed higher. He said that Jesus didn't need to come, even though that was His plan. So the centurion's faith allowed Jesus to work in a higher way. We can tap into a higher level of power in Jesus by raising our standard of faith.

Don't limit yourself because Jesus never did.

Jesus and the Woman with Perfume:

The next thing that I want to cover is the story of Jesus and the weeping woman. To give some backstory, Jesus was having dinner with a Pharisee, and while having dinner, a woman came and started washing Jesus's feet with her tears.

> ***And there was a woman in the city who was a sinner; and when she learned that He was reclining at the table in the Pharisee's house, she brought an alabaster vial of perfume, and standing behind Him at His feet, weeping, she began to wet His feet with her tears, and kept wiping them with the hair of her head, and kissing His feet and anointing them with the perfume.***
>
> ***Luke 7:37-38***

When the Pharisee saw this happening, he asked Jesus why He was letting the woman do this. So, in typical Jesus fashion, He decided to use a parable to explain.

And Jesus answered him, "Simon, I have something to say to you." And he replied, "Say it, Teacher." "A moneylender had two debtors: one owed five hundred denarii, and the other fifty. When they were unable to repay, he graciously forgave them both. So which of them will love him more?" Simon answered and said, "I suppose the one whom he forgave more." And He said to him, "You have judged correctly." Turning toward the woman, He said to Simon, "Do you see this woman? I entered your house; you gave Me no water for My feet, but she has wet My feet with her tears and wiped them with her hair. You gave Me no kiss; but she, since the time I came in, has not ceased to kiss My feet. You did not anoint My head with oil, but she anointed My feet with perfume. For this reason I say to you, her sins, which are many, have been forgiven, for she loved much; but he who is forgiven little, loves little." Then He said to her, "Your sins have been forgiven." Those who were reclining at the table with Him began to say to themselves, "Who

> *is this man who even forgives sins?"*
> *And He said to the woman, "Your faith*
> *has saved you; go in peace."*

Luke 7:40-50

Jesus gives the Pharisee that answer by explaining how if a person is forgiven of much, whether that be of offense or debt, then they are going to love the person that they forgave them much more. Now to me, this has always made sense, but what doesn't make sense is that what the woman did was considered faith by Jesus. Now how does it make sense that washing someone's feet is an act of faith? Here is what the Lord showed me. It was her faith in who He was that caused her to worship Him. You see, if we had true and real faith, we would worship the Lord like this woman did. We would spare no expense in worshiping Him, just as the woman did when she poured out her costly perfume on His feet. This ties in well with the last teaching because both have to do with getting a revelation of who Jesus really is. When we know Jesus as the Son of God, then we would actually worship Him in a real way. The other thing we can learn from this passage is that Jesus is drawing a connection between love and forgiveness. The more you are forgiven, the more you love. Now if my love of Jesus depends on how much I have been forgiven of, how can I actually grow my love of Jesus? Repent! That's right, if we repent before God, we will be forgiven of more. Then, in turn, our love of Jesus will grow, and we can learn to worship Him as He truly is. And this type of worship is also an act of faith because it was this very act that led Jesus to say, "your faith has saved you; go in peace."

Jesus and the Storm:

The story of Jesus and the storm is a classic example of Jesus and His authority. But in terms of breaking it down and finding a lesson of faith, it can be challenging. With that being said, I want to share with you what the Lord has given me through one of my favorite teachers, Kevin Zadai. I was hesitant to put his teaching in this book due to the fact that I am using another man's teaching in a book that I am writing, but I think it is too important to leave out when studying faith. So with that being said, let's check it out.

> ***Now on one of those days Jesus and His disciples got into a boat, and He said to them, "Let us go over to the other side of the lake." So they launched out. But as they were sailing along He fell asleep; and a fierce gale of wind***

descended on the lake, and they began to be swamped and to be in danger. They came to Jesus and woke Him up, saying, "Master, Master, we are perishing!" And He got up and rebuked the wind and the surging waves, and they stopped, and it became calm. And He said to them, "Where is your faith?" They were fearful and amazed, saying to one another, "Who then is this, that He commands even the winds and the water, and they obey Him?"

Luke 8:22-25

So on the surface level, it seems there isn't too much to glean from this passage. It looks like Jesus is just being mystical again and speaks to a storm. He then asks His disciples where their faith is, presuming that they were the ones who were supposed to speak to the storm. But something about this situation is that the lesson of faith here is that Jesus told the disciples that they were going to go over to the other side of the lake. Now, at first glance, this just seems like Jesus is making a plan and letting His disciples know about it. But the important thing that you might be missing is the fact that when Jesus did something, it was only because the Father told Him to do it. Jesus had such a close relationship with the Father that He went to the Father for everything. Jesus confirms this in the book of John, when He says,

> ***Therefore Jesus answered and was saying to them, "Truly, truly, I say to you, the Son can do nothing of Himself, unless it is something He sees the Father doing; for whatever the Father does, these things the Son also does in like manner.***

John 5:19

This is why Jesus had such confidence in going across that sea, to the point where He had fallen asleep in the boat while a storm was going on. Now, it is debatable on whether Jesus was thinking if His disciples would calm the storm themselves, or if He was wanting them to not worry about the storm. Either way, we can learn something awesome about faith. Jesus had faith, not in Himself but in the Father. He trusted that if the Father told Him to do something, it would be successful. So when He told His disciples that they were going over to the other side, He had full confidence that it would happen. Then when the storm came, Jesus knew that a storm couldn't stop the will of God, so He rebuked the winds. We can walk in that same kind of faith, but we need to build our relationship with God. Not only is it going to take trust, but it will also mean you have to learn how to hear what God is saying to you. If you know that God is telling you to cross a proverbial lake in your life, then you can be confident that you will be able to cross it. This is because God will never give you a mission that you can achieve. Now you may not achieve it because you didn't seek Him or rely on Him, but that is another matter entirely. The thing to know is that if God gives you a plan, then it will happen. We can tap into that rebuking prayer when something happens in our life that is contrary to what the Lord has told you. That is what Jesus did in this scenario. The important thing to learn here is that when the Lord tells you what to do and where to go, you can be sure that it will happen. And the second thing to know is that if you want to walk in that kind of confidence and security in the Lord, then you need to bring every decision you make to the Lord. If Jesus didn't only do what the Father told Him, why would He have confidence in His mission. I wouldn't! If you are doing your own thing and not walking in the counsel of the Lord, don't expect that the Lord will give you success.

Lessons from Jesus

Jesus and the Crowd:

The next story that we are going to cover is the story of the woman with the issue of blood. Now this story can teach us a lot about faith and also about seeing discrepancies in prayer. Let's check it out.

> ***And He went off with him; and a large crowd was following Him and pressing in on Him. A woman who had had a hemorrhage for twelve years, and had endured much at the hands of many physicians, and had spent all that she had and was not helped at all, but rather had grown worse— after hearing about Jesus, she came up in the crowd behind Him and touched His cloak. For she thought, "If I just touch His garments, I will get well." Immediately the flow of her blood was dried up; and she felt in her body that she was healed of her affliction. Immediately Jesus, perceiving in Himself that the power proceeding from Him had gone forth, turned around in the crowd and said, "Who touched My garments?" And His disciples said to Him, "You see the crowd***

> *pressing in on You, and You say, 'Who touched Me?'" And He looked around to see the woman who had done this. But the woman fearing and trembling, aware of what had happened to her, came and fell down before Him and told Him the whole truth. And He said to her, "Daughter, your faith has made you well; go in peace and be healed of your affliction."*
>
> **Mark 5:24-34**

I chose to use the passage from Mark instead of the passage from Luke because I believe it provides better insight into learning about faith. This is because we get to see how the woman was thinking in the moment. One thing that the Lord has shown me from this passage is that we should have the same mentality that the woman had. The woman said, "If I touch even his garments, I will be made well." This provides us a behind-the-scenes look at her faith. She had such faith that she told herself that she only needed to touch the garments of Jesus to be healed; this is after years of receiving treatment from physicians. All the while, people seemed to be crowding Jesus, assuming they, too, wanted some miracles for themselves. Yet out of all that crowd, it was only this woman who was healed. So much so that Jesus could actually feel the power leave Him without His consent. Think about that! This woman had so much faith in Jesus that without Jesus knowing what was going on, she got healed! This is profound because it shows us the power that is within the very being of Jesus, and it shows us how much our faith is required for drawing out that power. You see, we hold the key to our healing. Jesus Himself is the power, but our faith is the key that unlocks it. The other thing that is important to note is that the woman didn't want hands laid on her, nor did she think she needed it. And it was true that she didn't need hands laid on her, but all she needed was to touch the garments of Jesus. Sometimes we make healing and provision more complicated than it needs to be because we assume what needs to be done. We think we need some famous minister to pray for us, or maybe we think we need to go on a long fast to get our healing. This can actually limit us in receiving because we are putting our faith in fasting and men rather than in God.

The Plowing Slave:

This next lesson that we will look at is about the parable that Jesus gave His disciples when they asked Him to increase their faith. So, if you want the basic answer to increasing one's faith, then this is the parable for you.

> *The apostles said to the Lord, "Increase our faith!" And the Lord said, "If you had faith like a mustard seed, you would say to this mulberry tree, 'Be uprooted and be planted in the sea'; and it would obey you. "Which of you, having a slave plowing or tending sheep, will say to him when he has come in from the field, 'Come immediately and sit down to eat'? But will he not say to him, 'Prepare something for me to eat, and properly clothe yourself and serve me while I eat and drink; and afterward you may eat and drink'? He does not thank the slave because he did the things which were commanded, does he? So you too, when you do all the things which are commanded you, say, 'We are unworthy slaves; we have done only that which we ought to have done.'"*
>
> *Luke 17:5-10*

Now, for a long time, I didn't understand this parable because I had separated it from the previous statement about faith. But if we look closely, we can see that this passage is a cohesive message about faith. First, His disciples cry out to Him and ask that they would receive greater faith. So we know that everything that follows would be teaching on faith. Jesus then tells His disciples that if they had faith like a mustard seed, they would be able to say to a mulberry tree, "Be uprooted and be planted in the sea." The thing to note and pay attention to here is that Jesus says that tree will obey **you**. That's right, when you have faith like a mustard seed, your prayers become commands. This can be an interesting but important way to change how you view prayer. Rather than prayer being only a petition, it is also acting as a type of command that you are giving. Then, Jesus tells His disciples that if anyone is to have a servant, and they come in from the field, should they not serve their master before eating? Now, if you are a little confused right now as to how this has anything to do with faith, don't be worried as I was too for a long time. Here is what the Lord has shown me. In this parable, we are the servant, and God is our master. We have been out in the field and have been working. Yet when we are called into the Master's house, we also have to serve Him there. Only then will we get to eat and drink. And all the while, the Master does not thank the slave for what he did because the slave did nothing other than what he should have done for his master. So we should also not expect to eat and drink the blessing of answered prayer if we don't do as we are supposed to. I know it can be hard to hear, but obedience is a key to having one's prayers answered. Even James talks about this in his letter.

> ***Therefore, confess your sins to one another, and pray for one another so that you may be healed. The effective prayer of a righteous man can accomplish much. Elijah was a man with a nature like ours, and he prayed earnestly that it would not rain, and it did not rain on the earth for three years and six months. Then he prayed again, and the sky poured rain and the earth produced its fruit.***
>
> ***James 5:16-18***

Obedience and righteousness are pieces of the puzzle when it comes to having our prayers answered.

Lessons from Jesus

Jesus and the Lepers:

This is one of my favorite pieces of Scripture that we can break down to learn about faith. I think it is important to learn from this one because it shows us an often overlooked part of faith. Let's check it out.

> *When He saw them, He said to them, "Go and show yourselves to the priests." And as they were going, they were cleansed. Now one of them, when he saw that he had been healed, turned back, glorifying God with a loud voice, and he fell on his face at His feet, giving thanks to Him. And he was a Samaritan. Then Jesus answered and said, "Were there not ten cleansed? But the nine—where are they? Was no one found who returned to give glory to God, except this foreigner?" And He said to him, "Stand up and go; your faith has made you well."*

Luke 17:14-19

The story of the lepers is that even though all of them were healed by Jesus, only one of them came back to give thanks to Him. This can teach us about how we are to relate to Jesus. When He comes into our lives and gives us salvation on the cross, we are to come and worship Him. And in any answered prayer or blessing given to us, we are to give thanks to God. Now most people think that, of course, God would want to be worshiped and thanked. And they have an attitude of seeing God as vain or prideful for desiring praise. But this is not the case, and, in fact, if anyone else was in the position of God, they would want the same thing! You see, God is a person. And just like any other person, He wants to be recognized for what He has done for you. If you gave someone a gift, you would expect them to say thank you. And think about the gift that Jesus gave us! He died on the cross and suffered the punishment that we deserved so that we could become part of the family of God. He is deserving and worthy of all our praise for eternity! I mean, think about it, imagine getting to be part of the most exclusive group in all of creation, the family of God. And no human there has gotten there based on merit but only because someone else bought their ticket. For eternity, we will sit in a place of privilege, all because God loved us enough to send His son to die for us. We need to be like that leper who was healed. And you know what Jesus says to that man? He tells Him that because He came back to give thanks, He was healed and that his faith has made him well. That means Jesus is making a connection to giving thanks and faith. If we really believed that Jesus died for us, we would always give Him thanks. When we properly recognize the blessings in our life as coming from God, we can put that on our list of faith. And we can look back on those for building our faith in the future. Thank you Jesus!

Jesus and the Parable of the Persistent Widow

The parable that we are going to go over next is one of my favorite parables because it is a perfect example of what I have learned in prayer from personal experience. Let's go over it.

> *Now He was telling them a parable to show that at all times they ought to pray and not to lose heart, saying, "In a certain city there was a judge who did not fear God and did not respect man. There was a widow in that city, and she kept coming to him, saying, 'Give me legal protection from my opponent.' For a while he was unwilling; but afterward he said to himself, 'Even though I do not fear God nor respect man, yet because this widow bothers me, I will give her legal protection, otherwise by*

continually coming she will wear me out.'" And the Lord said, "Hear what the unrighteous judge *said; now, will not God bring about justice for His elect who cry to Him day and night, and will He delay long over them? I tell you that He will bring about justice for them quickly. However, when the Son of Man comes, will He find faith on the earth?"

Luke 18:1-8

In this parable, we see that our prayers to God are compared to a widow seeking legal protection from an unrighteous judge. In the parable, we see that the only reason that the widow got protection from the judge is because of her persistence. In my experience, this parable is probably one of the most important parables when it comes to praying. In my life, I have learned to be persistent and consistent in my prayers to God. Sometimes I have had prayers that have not been answered for months, yet because I persisted in prayer, I saw the answer. When anyone asks me about prayer, I always come to this parable and this truth. If you are consistent in your prayers, you will see them answered. This persistence is actually equated with faith.

And this is because it takes a lot of faith to continue pressing into that prayer when you haven't seen any fruit in it. It is like a person in a mine. They know that there is gold in the mine, they are guaranteed it. But they don't know how long it will take to mine out the gold. Maybe they try to mine out the gold for a week, maybe two, or maybe they try for a whole month. But after not seeing any gold, they give up and convince themselves that there isn't any gold in the mine. But in reality, there is gold! They just didn't have the endurance to reach it. This is the case with prayer. God gives you the guarantee that there is an answer, but He never guarantees when that answer will come.

You have to keep this persistence and faith to see that answered prayer. The fact that you even get down on your knees to request something from God is an act of faith. Be persistent, and you will see results!

Jesus and the Blind Man:

This next story is about the importance of perseverance and boldness when approaching Christ. Let's check it out!

> ***Then they *came to Jericho. And as He was leaving Jericho with His disciples***

and a large crowd, a blind beggar named Bartimaeus, the son of Timaeus, was sitting by the road. When he heard that it was Jesus the Nazarene, he began to cry out and say, "Jesus, Son of David, have mercy on me!" Many were sternly telling him to be quiet, but he kept crying out all the more, "Son of David, have mercy on me!" And Jesus stopped and said, "Call him here." So they *called the blind man, saying to him, "Take courage, stand up! He is calling for you." Throwing aside his cloak, he jumped up and came to Jesus. And answering him, Jesus said, "What do you want Me to do for you?" And the blind man said to Him, "Rabboni, I want to regain my sight!" And Jesus said to him, "Go; your faith has made you well." Immediately he regained his sight and began following Him on the road.

Mark 10:46-52

Before I start to break down this passage, I would like to give some credit to Kevin Zadai, as what I learned from this passage is partly from him. He is a fantastic teacher and is truly led by God. I would highly recommend his work to anyone, including you. So with that being said, let's continue with the breakdown. One of the most important things to notice is how the blind beggar addresses Jesus. He gives Him the title of Son of David. This is a reference to the Messiah, so we can see that the blind man "saw" Jesus as the Messiah. This is interesting because it paints an interesting picture of contrast between those who can see yet do not discern who Jesus really is and the fact that a blind man can "see" Jesus for who He really is. The other thing to note is that even though the crowd was trying to get him to be quiet, he didn't listen to them. The man couldn't care less about what the crowd had to say. So Jesus hears the man's cries and brings him forward to ask the man what he wants. The man then replies that he would want to have his eyesight restored. Jesus then grants this and heals the man's eyes, but he also says that the man's faith has made him well. But where was his faith? It was in his calling out to Jesus and not allowing the crowd to control him. A lot of times, we can get caught up with how other people want us to be. There are many societal pressures that all humans face. But real faith is not backing down from your seeking of Jesus just because the crowd is trying to silence you. The less we care about the crowd, and the more we care about Jesus, the better. If we can do that, then we can start to live in victory in Christ and have all our prayers answered.

> *As Jesus went on from there, two blind men followed Him, crying out, "Have mercy on us, Son of David!" When He entered the house, the blind men came up to Him, and Jesus *said to them, "Do you believe that I am able to do this?" They *said to Him, "Yes, Lord." Then He touched their eyes, saying, "It shall be done to you according to your faith." And their eyes were opened. And Jesus sternly warned them: "See that no one knows about this!"*
>
> *Matthew 9:27-30*

Now we have a similar story if not the same story in a different account in the book of Matthew. Now there still is the same theme of the blind men calling Jesus the son of David, but what I want to point out here is the sincerity of the blind men. Throughout the New Testament, Jesus had many instances of supernatural discernment, whether that was discerning the thoughts of the Pharisees or the thoughts of His disciples. When these blind men came up to Jesus, they truly knew that Jesus was able to heal them.

Because if they didn't, Jesus would have known. I only bring up this version of the story because I want to ask you a question. Do you believe Jesus can do this? Do you really believe Jesus can bring your miracle? We should take time to meditate on this question and ask ourselves if we are seeing Jesus in His full reality.

Jesus and the Paralytic:

The story of Jesus and the paralytic has always been an interesting one for me, mostly because there were some people who broke through a roof just to see Jesus. But we are actually gonna go over that in the breakdown. Let's get started!

> ***Being unable to get to Him because of the crowd, they removed the roof above Him; and when they had dug an opening, they let down the pallet on which the paralytic was lying. And Jesus seeing their faith *said to the paralytic, "Son, your sins are forgiven." But some of the scribes were sitting there and reasoning in their hearts, "Why does this man speak that way? He is blaspheming; who can forgive sins but God alone?" Immediately Jesus, aware***

> *in His spirit that they were reasoning that way within themselves, *said to them, "Why are you reasoning about these things in your hearts? Which is easier, to say to the paralytic, 'Your sins are forgiven'; or to say, 'Get up, and pick up your pallet and walk'? But so that you may know that the Son of Man has authority on earth to forgive sins"—He *said to the paralytic, "I say to you, get up, pick up your pallet and go home."*

Mark 2:4-11

The story starts out with Jesus teaching a large crowd in Capernaum, and there was a group of people who had a paralytic friend. They had heard of Jesus and His healings, so they brought their friend to see Him in Capernaum, only to find that they cannot reach Him because of the crowd. But this doesn't stop them; instead, they decide to make their own way and break through the roof to see Jesus. When Jesus sees the paralytic, He tells the paralytic that His sins are forgiven and that He can get up and walk. The paralytic is healed, and people praise Jesus because of this miracle. Now this should be the end of the story but I want to point out some small details that can teach us a lot. First, is that when it came to getting their friend healed, they didn't hold back. They went so far as to destroy the house that Jesus was in just to see Him. They quite literally had a breakthrough to get healing. The second thing that is important to note is that when Jesus was looking for faith, the Scripture says that Jesus saw their faith. That means that it was the collective faith of the paralytic and the friends. This is the perfect picture of praying and believing for other people. Your collective faith is what grants the healing. So next time we are praying for another person, we should be thinking of how in a way, we are carrying that person on a pallet to get healed by Jesus.

Jesus Walks on Water:

Peter said to Him, "Lord, if it is You, command me to come to You on the water." And He said, "Come!" And Peter got out of the boat, and walked on the water and came toward Jesus. But seeing the wind, he became frightened, and beginning to sink, he cried out, "Lord, save me!" Immediately Jesus stretched out His hand and took hold of him, and *said to him, "You

> *of little faith, why did you doubt?" When they got into the boat, the wind stopped. And those who were in the boat worshiped Him, saying, "You are certainly God's Son!"*

Matthew 14:28-33

Most Christians and many secular people know about the story of Jesus walking on water. It is so popular and well known that there have even been magicians like Chris Angel who have created visual effects that try to replicate this miracle. But if we break down this passage, we can find some super interesting pieces of information that can help us in our faith walk. The first one that the Lord has shown me is that the reason that Peter started to sink into the sea was because he took his eyes off of Jesus. Instead of looking at the man who was walking on water, he looked at the storm around him. Imagine being in a situation where you are literally walking on water by the power of God, and you start worrying about a storm. I mean, talk about being distracted. But the lesson here is that if you can keep your eyes on Jesus and not worry about the storm around you, then you will be able to walk on the water with Jesus. The second thing is that after Jesus got back into the boat, His disciples started to worship Him as the Son of God. Now this would be the correct thing to do, but didn't Peter also walk on the water? Now I am not trying to say that Peter was on the same level as Jesus, but what I am trying to suggest is that maybe we have limited ourselves too much. I mean, Jesus tells us that we can cast mountains into the sea with our words if we have enough faith. Some part of you has to start to realize your potential in Christ. If Christ tells you that you can walk on water, then you can. Walk in the power of Jesus's words. And this is not from any esoteric idea of what man can become but rather from the very words of Jesus. He told us that not only will we do the same works that He did, but we will do even greater things.

Jesus and the Humble Woman:

The story that we are going to cover in this next section is the story of the woman with the demon-possessed daughter. Now this story can be confusing to some because of how Jesus speaks to this woman. But I want to show you that we can learn a lot from this woman when it comes to faith, and I would like to suggest that maybe Jesus was speaking to the woman in a way that tested her.

> **But He answered and said, "I was sent only to the lost sheep of the house of**

> *Israel." But she came and began to bow down before Him, saying, "Lord, help me!" And He answered and said, "It is not good to take the children's bread and throw it to the dogs." But she said, "Yes, Lord; but even the dogs feed on the crumbs which fall from their masters' table." Then Jesus said to her, "O woman, your faith is great; it shall be done for you as you wish." And her daughter was healed at once.*
>
> *Matthew 15:24-28*

At first, we can see that Jesus tells the woman that He has only come for the lost sheep of the house of Israel. For those who do not understand, the "lost sheep of the house of Israel" are those of the tribes of Israel who have lost their relationship with God. But even after hearing this and knowing that she was not considered one of the lost sheep of Israel, as she was a Gentile and not part of the tribes of Israel, she still comes and bows before Jesus. You see, she didn't care that she wasn't considered one of the lost sheep; all she cared about was getting the help she needed. Jesus then tells her that it is wrong to give the children's bread to dogs, implying that the lost sheep of Israel are children, and the Gentiles are dogs.

But even this does not deter the woman, and instead of walking away offended, she humbled herself and took up the title of dog. After this, Jesus compliments her and tells her that she is a woman of great faith. He then grants her wish by healing her daughter from demon possession. Here is the thing to learn, though. Jesus told her that He was only sent to the lost sheep of the house of Israel, yet this woman was able to go past that and get Jesus to help her. Now how does she do that? She humbles herself before Him. She called Him Lord and bowed down before Him. When she was essentially called lesser, she accepted this title and still asked for help. This is the attitude that we need to have. Jesus called this attitude faith. When we approach God, we need to be humble. And when God wants to humble us, just as Jesus wanted to humble that woman, we need to accept it. Humility is essential and is one of the most important aspects of a strong faith.

Jesus and His Hometown:

This next story is about the lesson that we can learn from when Jesus came back to his hometown of Nazareth. This story can teach us a lot about unbelief and how Jesus isn't the one restricting us, but rather we restrict ourselves.

> *Jesus went out from there and *came into His hometown; and His disciples *followed Him. When the Sabbath came, He began to teach in the synagogue; and the many listeners were astonished, saying, "Where did this man get these things, and what is this wisdom given to Him, and such miracles as these performed by His hands? Is not this the carpenter, the son of Mary, and brother of James and Joses and Judas and Simon? Are not His sisters here with us?" And they took offense at Him. Jesus said to them, "A prophet is not without honor except in his hometown and among his own relatives and in his own household." And He could do no miracle there except that He laid His hands on a few sick people and healed them. And He wondered at their unbelief. And He was going around the villages teaching.*
>
> **Mark 6:1-6**

The first thing to notice in this story is that when Jesus came back to His hometown to teach in the synagogue, the people were astonished by His teaching.

They knew that what He was saying was profound and was good, but they couldn't see past the fact that they knew Jesus as a kid. They may have seen Jesus grow up in the physical, but they didn't see Him grow up spiritually. And that can be the case with your own development and growth. If people do not have discernment, they won't be able to see your spiritual progress and your relationship with the Lord. But because of how the people of Nazareth viewed Jesus, Jesus was unable to heal people and perform miracles. Here is what we can learn from this story: not only will people not recognize your spiritual growth, especially if they have known you for a long time. And the second thing to know is that Jesus was unable to heal people because of their lack of faith. We see Jesus as the Son of God and all-powerful, but the one thing that stopped Him was unbelief.

Now, I don't know why this is the case, but if unbelief can restrict Jesus, then belief is the thing that allows Him access to move in your life. We have to understand that God may have plans for your life that He wants to accomplish, but if we are in unbelief, He won't be able to do them. It is up to you in the end if you want God to move.

Jesus and the Unbelieving Believer:

and whenever it seizes him, it slams him to the ground and he foams at the mouth, and grinds his teeth and stiffens out. I told Your disciples to cast it out, and they could not do it." And He *answered them and *said, "O unbelieving generation, how long shall I be with you? How long shall I put up with you? Bring him to Me!" They brought the boy to Him. When he saw Him, immediately the spirit threw him into a convulsion, and falling to the ground, he began rolling around and foaming at the mouth. And He asked his father, "How long has this been happening to him?" And he said, "From childhood. It has often thrown him both into the fire and into the water to destroy him. But if You can do anything, take pity on us and help us!" And Jesus said to him, "'If You can?' All things are possible to him who believes." Immediately the boy's father cried out and said, "I do believe; help my unbelief."

Mark 9:18-24

Lessons from Jesus

This story is about finding a discrepancy or disappointment when praying for something or seeking something. A man was trying to have his son delivered from a demon, and when he went to the disciples, they were unable to free the boy. When Jesus came to the city, the man approached Him and asked why His disciples were unable to cast out the demon. Jesus then asks the father a question about how long the demon has been oppressing the boy, to which the father responds that it has been happening from childhood. The man also asks that if Jesus can do anything, then He should pity the boy and free him from the demon. Jesus then comments about the man's "if you can" statement and tells the man that all things are possible with God. The man then responds with "I do believe; help my unbelief." Now this is the statement and part of the story that I really wanted to go over with you guys. Here we have a man who is not only proclaiming that he does believe but that he also has unbelief. How is this possible, you might ask? Well, if we view it as a black-and-white situation, where there is either unbelief and belief, then this man is a paradox. He is either one or the other.

But I would say that when it comes to faith, there are levels and depths beyond a black-and-white scenario. You might have the faith to make Jesus your Lord and Savior, but do you have the faith to get prayers answered? What the man was trying to tell

Jesus was that though he believed, there was a part of him that couldn't go far enough to say that Jesus is willing and able to heal his son. i believe that this is because people don't want to put their faith to the test. Because if we test it, and it fails, we will have to deal with that reality and reconsider what we believe. But it is a lot easier to never test what you believe and therefore never have to deal with a sense of loss or confusion. This is exactly where the enemy wants you to live in. He doesn't want you to pray because he knows prayer works.

The enemy would rather have you living a powerless Christian life without prayer. So he plans on bringing delay to every prayer you have so that you start to develop doubt. Or maybe he convinces you of the lie that praying doesn't work because if it happens, it was always going to happen, and if it doesn't, then it is only proof of how prayer doesn't work. C. S. Lewis calls this the "heads, I win; tails, you lose" scenario in his book, 'The Screwtape Letters'. It is essentially a situation where you never win. There are plenty of ways in which the enemy can take away from your prayer life, but we need to come against those attacks. What this man was asking Jesus was to help him with his level of faith, and I think we all need to ask Jesus for another level of faith. So we can use that faith we have now to have our prayer answered for more faith in the future. Faith is like a seed that can grow into something huge. That is what Jesus is talking about when He speaks of faith as a mustard seed.

So let's work on deepening our level of faith in God.

Jesus and the Fig Tree:

This will be the last teaching of Jesus that we go over in this chapter, and I believe this may be the best teaching that Jesus has given us. It is about truly having faith and trust in God when you pray.

> *On the next day, when they had left Bethany, He became hungry. Seeing at a distance a fig tree in leaf, He went to see if perhaps He would find anything on it; and when He came to it, He found nothing but leaves, for it was not the season for figs. He said to it, "May no one ever eat fruit from you again!" And His disciples were listening.*
>
> *Mark 11:12-14*

The story starts out with Jesus leaving the town of Bethany, and while He is leaving, He becomes hungry and starts to look for food. While looking for food, He sees a fig tree off in the distance and goes over to grab Himself something to eat. But when He gets there, the tree doesn't have any fruit on it. So Jesus curses the tree and says to it, "May no one ever eat fruit from you again!." While this happened, His disciples were listening to Him. Later on, they came back to this tree.

> *Being reminded, Peter *said to Him, "Rabbi, look, the fig tree which You cursed has withered." And Jesus *answered saying to them, "Have faith in God. Truly I say to you, whoever says to this mountain, 'Be taken up and cast into the sea,' and does not doubt in his heart, but believes that what he says is going to happen, it will be granted him. Therefore I say to you, all things for which you pray and ask, believe that you have received them, and they will be granted you. Whenever you stand praying, forgive, if you have anything against anyone, so that your Father who is in heaven will also forgive you your transgressions.*
>
> *Mark 11:21-25*

Lessons from Jesus

The disciples notice that the tree that Jesus cursed has actually withered and is dead. They tell Jesus this, and Jesus responds by telling them to have faith in God. He teaches them that if they ask for it, then it will happen. But what He doesn't say is that it will happen instantly. We have to believe that if we say something will happen, then it will inevitably happen. This, of course, can only happen when we ask in the name of Jesus, but we must know that sometimes prayers don't get answered quickly. We have to believe in our hearts that we have already received them because we have to be patient and long-suffering. Another way to pray and believe that we have received it is to act out our belief. If you prayed that you would get a new house, then start packing. If you prayed that you would receive that new job, start preparing yourself for that new role. Act out your belief. And the last lesson from this story is that forgiveness is a huge key when it comes to having prayers answered. Unforgiveness will actually block your prayers from being answered. That is why Jesus says that whenever we stand praying, we need to forgive all those who we have held in unforgiveness so that our Father in heaven will forgive us our transgressions. Well, now that we have covered most, if not all the most important places in the gospel where Jesus talks about faith, in the next chapter, we will summarize what we learned. Let's go!

Builiding Your Tower

Chapter 9

How We Can Apply the Lessons of Faith

Now that we have gone over many lessons of faith from both the Gospels and the Old Testament, it is time to put them into action. This chapter will be dedicated to covering some topics on the implementation of these faith lessons. The first thing to note is there are generally going to be two categories that these lessons of faith will fall into, the practical methods of increasing one's faith and the type of growth that only God can give us. But even in the second category, there is still a requirement from us to act, and we will talk about that later. First, let's go over some of the lessons that we learned for practical faith-building.

Practical Lessons:

Lessons from David	1. Standing on the covenant of the blood of Jesus: Just like David stood in the covenant of Abraham, we, too, can stand on the covenant that we have through the blood of Jesus. We don't fight from the physical but rather from a place of spiritual strength in God. So what does that look like? It looks like you solving your problems with God and not trusting in the arm of man (Jer. 17:5).

2. Praying in the name of the Lord Jesus: When David spoke to Goliath, he told Goliath what he was going to do to him. He let Goliath know that he would be taking his life and then his head. David spoke for the Lord because he knew he was representing the Lord when he went out to fight for His honor. David didn't fight for himself but for the Lord. We can also be like David when we pray in the name of Jesus. We are making a stand just like David because we are representing the Lord on the battlefield of prayer.
3. *In that day you will not question Me about anything. Truly, truly, I say to you, if you ask the Father for anything in My name, He will give it to you. John 16:23*

Lessons from Moses	1. Petition to the breaking point: When Moses came before Pharaoh to ask for the freedom of the Israelites, he already knew it would take multiple attempts before Pharaoh would let them go. And we also know that when we pray, it is not going to always happen on the first prayer. But we need to have a mentality of praying till our blessing is released, just as Moses continued to petition Pharaoh till the Israelites were set free.

2 Don't run away from the staff the Lord gave you: When studying Moses we found that the staff that he used to shepherd sheep in the wilderness would be the same staff that led Israel out into the wilderness. The staff represents what the Lord had given him to prepare him for his mission. But when Moses threw down his staff at the command of the Lord, he fled from it. Don't flee from the tools that the Lord has given you! One day, that staff will be turned into a serpent, and you will use it for the glory of the Lord. So don't be afraid of it.

Lessons from Joshua	1. Our time in prayer is time around the wall: We learned from Joshua that our prayers are just like when Israel circled the walls of Jericho. Though, outwardly, it looked pointless, if not even madness, it was working to tear down the walls of Jericho. So when we are praying, we have to remember that even though it can feel like nothing is happening, the Lord is moving on our behalf.

Lessons from Ruth	1. Love and obedience: Ruth taught us the importance of selfless love. She is a prime example of the love that God has for us, that God stayed with us when there was no benefit to Him. He blessed us with His Son Jesus. And now we should walk in that same
Lessons from Noah	1. Wait till the Lord says "Go": Noah was a man of patience and trust. We learned from him about the importance of not using your own wisdom and understanding but rather to trust in the Lord and His timing. We need to learn from Him and trust in the Lord's timing. Don't leave that ark until the Lord tells you to.

Lessons from Daniel	1. Prioritize your relationship with God: We learned from Daniel that our relationship with the Lord should be our highest priority. It was only Daniel's relationship with the Lord that saved him from the lions. And we should also walk in the same way. If we learn to prioritize God, we will have the same favor that Daniel had.

2. The king fasted and prayed when he had exhausted the options for Daniel. But we should fast and pray as our first move when wanting to solve problems. As Christians, we operate as ambassadors to God, so let us actually use the power of God in our lives
3. We learned from Gabriel that the reason for delay in our prayer is that there are spiritual forces at work that are hindering our prayers. Gabriel could not have gotten to Daniel if it wasn't for Michael, the archangel, coming to help. This shows us that a real battle is going on right now that we cannot see. Don't give up if your prayers are taking a while to be answered, but stand firm in prayer and know that it will be a battle.

Lessons from Gideon	1. We learned that we need to hear from the Lord and follow His commands; no more coming back for an answer you already received. A servant doesn't ask twice, and a soldier doesn't ask twice. We are called to be obedient children of God!

This next section will cover lessons that can only really be developed in us by the Lord and have little to do with how we act; mostly because we need to learn how to react to things, and that takes training from our heavenly Father. So let's check out this next list.

Lessons from David	1. We learned when reading about David that before the Lord had brought him to face down and kill Goliath, he had already killed both a lion and bear. This means that the Lord was preparing David for something bigger in his life, but he was using smaller challenges to work up to that. The Lord does that in our lives as well. We should pray that the Lord would prepare us just as He prepared David.

Lessons from Moses	1. The story of Moses taught us that the Lord tells us who we are; Moses was too caught up in his own weakness to notice the glory and power of God. Let the power of God overcome your weakness, and He will transform you into something new and amazing. Moses didn't believe that he could speak well, but at the end of his life, he was giving speeches and speaking to the multitudes of Israel. God is the potter, and you are the clay. So let Him do His work in making you amazing! We need to pray that we would be shaped to fulfill the destiny and plan that He has for us, and that we would be conformed to the image of Christ.

	2. We also learned that when we are struggling to walk in the path that the Lord has for us, sometimes the Lord will bring people to help us. We need to surround ourselves with strong believers so we can overcome our fear.
Lessons from Esther	1. We learned from Esther that just as she was granted favor by the king, we, too, are granted favor by our king. We need to learn to come boldly before the throne of Christ and ask the Lord to take out the plans of the enemy in our lives. We should pray that our relationship would grow with God but also that we would have a revelation of how much He loves us.

Lessons from Ruth	1. We learned from Ruth that selfless love will take you very far in favor with the Lord. If we desire favor and blessing in our lives, then we need to pray that we, too, walk in selfless love, just as Ruth did, and just as Christ did for us.
Lessons from Noah	1. We learned from Noah that patience and listening is an important part of walking in faith. If we can't listen, how will we be able to receive a command from the Lord? And if we can't be patient, how can we actually walk out that plan? We need to pray for both patience and discernment of what the Lord is speaking to us.

Lessons from Gideon	1. As we saw from the story of Gideon, double-mindedness and fear can be a huge cause of stumbling. If we want to transition from a Gideon to a David, we need to pray that our fear would be replaced with courage and our doubt would be replaced with faith (1 John 4:18).

Now that we have gone over all the lessons that we learned from the Old Testament, let's transition to the lessons that we learned from Jesus.

Jesus and the Centurion	1. The lesson of the centurion is that he saw Jesus for who He really was. While the rest of the world saw Him as a teacher, this man saw Jesus as one with great authority. He saw Jesus as one who was under God and, therefore, was over creation. We need to pray that we have a revelation of who Jesus really is so we can have the faith that this man had. Jesus marveled at this kind of faith.

Jesus and the Woman with Perfume	1. We learned from the woman with the perfume that the more we are forgiven, the more we love Jesus. So let us be forgiven more by repenting more, so that we can grow in our love of Jesus. But don't dwell on what the Lord has freed you from but rather reach forward to the new level of holiness in Christ.
Jesus and the Storm	1. We learned that we can have confidence and faith in the Lord and His plan. But we also know that this kind of confidence can only come because we are walking in God's plan for our lives.

Jesus and the Crowd	1. What we learned from the woman with the issue of blood is that faith is the key that allows us access to the power of God. It was the woman's faith that drew out the power from Jesus without His consent.
Jesus and the Parable of the Plowing Slave	1. We learned that if you want to eat or have our prayer answered, then we need to have been working in the field for God. Only then will we receive our reward.
Jesus and the Lepers	1. The lepers taught us that part of a strong faith in recognizing your Savior is by honestly worshiping Him and giving Him the credit.

Jesus and the Persistent Widow	1. If we are persistent in prayer, this is accounted to us as faith! Be consistent in your prayers and remember that God promised an answer but never promised when.
Jesus and the Blind Man	1. The blind man taught us that we need to have a revelation of who Jesus really is as the Son of God and that we need to press on past the voices in the world that tell us to stop seeking Him.
Jesus and the Paralytic	1. The paralytic taught us that we can bring the sick to Jesus by our collective faith and that we need to stand with those who can't stand for themselves.

Jesus and His Hometown	1. We learned from the people of Nazareth that Jesus literally was unable to perform miracles because of their lack of faith. This means that your lack of faith could be the cause of unanswered prayers. Faith is the key that unlocks the power of God.
Jesus and the Unbelieving Believer	1. We learned from the people of Nazareth that Jesus literally was unable to perform miracles because of their lack of faith. This means that your lack of faith could be the cause of unanswered prayers. Faith is the key that unlocks the power of God.

Jesus and the Fig Tree	1. The story of the fig tree taught us the importance of believing that what you pray will happen, no matter the timeline. This is one of the most important lessons that we can learn.

Before we finish this book, I want to share one more lesson with you guys that the Lord has shown me. This lesson comes from a story in the book of Mark. I got this insight from the Lord during my own personal reading, outside of studying for this book. But I thought I would share what I learned from the Lord because I think it shows the place where I want people to end up after reading and applying these principles. Let's check it out.

> *Immediately Jesus made His disciples get into the boat and go ahead of Him to the other side to Bethsaida, while He Himself was sending the crowd away. After bidding them farewell, He left for the mountain to pray. When it was evening, the boat was in the middle of the sea, and He was alone on the land.*

> *Seeing them straining at the oars, for the wind was against them, at about the fourth watch of the night He *came to them, walking on the sea; and He intended to pass by them.*

Mark 6:45-48

So after praying and asking the Lord to show me something in His Word, I started to read in the book of Mark. As I was reading in Mark, there was one specific part of that passage above that stood out to me. Now I had read this passage many times before, but what the Lord pointed out to me this time is that when Jesus was walking on the water, He intended to pass by His struggling disciples. That's right, Jesus the man of love was intending to let His disciples struggle in the storm, and He was gonna walk the rest of the way to the other side of the lake. Now when I saw this, I was very confused, so I kept on reading to hopefully find an answer.

> *But when they saw Him walking on the sea, they supposed that it was a ghost, and cried out; for they all saw Him and were terrified. But immediately He spoke with them and *said to them, "Take courage; it is I, do not*

> *be afraid." Then He got into the boat with them, and the wind stopped; and they were utterly astonished, for they had not gained any insight from the incident of the loaves, but their heart was hardened.*
>
> *Mark 6:49-52*

Now, when they saw Jesus walking on water, they were predictably amazed and afraid. They thought that Jesus was a ghost, but Jesus told them not to be afraid. So Jesus got on the boat and calmed the winds, to their astonishment. But the Scripture says that they were utterly astonished, not because Jesus just walked on water and stopped a storm, but because they had not gained any insight into the loaves. So this means that had they gotten the insight from the loaves, they would have not been astonished. When I saw this, I immediately flipped back to the story of the loaves to see if I could get the insight that they missed.

> *But He answered them, "You give them something to eat!" And they *said to Him, "Shall we go and spend two hundred denarii on bread and give them something to eat?" And He *said to*

> *them, "How many loaves do you have? Go look!" And when they found out, they *said, "Five, and two fish." And He commanded them all to sit down by groups on the green grass. They sat down in groups of hundreds and of fifties. And He took the five loaves and the two fish, and looking up toward heaven, He blessed the food and broke the loaves and He kept giving them to the disciples to set before them; and He divided up the two fish among them all.*
>
> **Mark 6:37-41**

When coming to this passage, I asked the Lord to show me the insight that the disciples missed. After asking, there was one thing that was pointed out to me. Jesus told His disciples to give the people something to eat. Knowing full well that they didn't have the food or money to feed all the people, but He asked them to feed them anyways. After they made some excuses to Him, Jesus took the loaves and fish that they had and prayed over them so that they could be broken and feed all the people. So here is the insight that the disciples missed. Not only had they missed that all things were possible with God, having seen thousands fed with only five loaves and two fish, but they also missed that Jesus was asking them to do it.

You see, when Jesus was walking on the water and intending to pass them, it was because He was wanting His disciples to calm the storm, just like when He asked His disciples to feed the people. He wants you to calm the storm and feed the people. And I want you to have the faith to do these things. I want God to transform you just like when He changed Peter. Right before Jesus died, Peter denied Christ. But after Peter received the Holy Spirit and started to lead the early church, He had the faith to lift up the paralytic and heal him in the name of Jesus. That is the kind of transformation that I want to see in you.

> ***But Peter said, "I do not possess silver and gold, but what I do have I give to you: In the name of Jesus Christ the Nazarene—walk!" And seizing him by the right hand, he raised him up; and immediately his feet and his ankles were strengthened. With a leap he stood upright and began to walk; and he entered the temple with them, walking and leaping and praising God.***
>
> ***Acts 3:6-8 NASB1995***

Hear and Obey

The last and most important thing that I want to share is that faith ultimately isn't about how it can benefit you. I know that there was a whole chapter in this book looking at the benefits of faith, but what is more important is obeying God. There are things that the Lord will ask you to do that have a bigger impact on the world than you will think. The ultimate objective of our lives should be to do what the Father has commanded. Your actions can affect the eternal destinies of those around you. It could mean the difference between someone spending their life in eternal torment without God or in eternal relationship in the paradise of heaven. This is your higher calling. Grow your faith, not because it can help you but because it will help others. Jesus is, again, the highest example of this. We know from the book of John that Jesus neither spoke anything nor did anything unless the Father told Him to.

> *Therefore Jesus answered and was saying to them, "Truly, truly, I say to you, the Son can do nothing of Himself, unless it is something He sees the Father doing; for whatever the Father does, these things the Son also does in like manner.*

John 5:19

Do you not believe that I am in the Father, and the Father is in Me? The words that I say to you I do not speak on My own initiative, but the Father abiding in Me does His works.

John 14:10

We need to get to that point in our lives. That is all that matters in the end. God sees things from a higher view point and vantage than you do. He can use your life better than anyone else. One time, the Lord showed me that He is so powerful and has such a perfect understanding of reality that if He wanted to, He could lead you to a specific spot on the earth where if you stomped your foot, it would cause an earthquake. I fully believe this revelation. Faith is about recognizing Jesus as King. He is your Lord, and you are called to obey Him. He can do great things with you if you can learn to listen and obey.

Now that we have recapped all the lessons from this book, I want to talk about how this will impact you in your life. We, as humans, and especially as Christians, have received a lot of teaching in our lives. Whether that is from school, church, or your parents, everything a human knows came from someone else.

But we all know that there are some things in our lives that we hear or read, and it goes in one ear and out the other. Like, for example, high school chemistry class. You learn about all these old men who discovered all these elements and laws about how to find an electron, but after the test, you couldn't care less about that information. In fact, you may never recall those things again because you were learning them just for a good grade in class.

But this teaching is different because it can be a tool and blessing that can forever change your life. And I don't say this to flatter myself for what I wrote. In fact, I'll be the first person to say that I don't want credit for this book. It is only because the Lord had grace on me and allowed me to receive this teaching that I can write this. It is not because I am better than anyone else or more intelligent, but simply because the Lord asked me to do this. That is it. So I am asking you to take some time to not only apply these principles but also pray about everything in this book. If something that was written doesn't sit right with you, take it to the Lord. In the end, I am not your savior nor your teacher, but Jesus fulfills those roles in your life. Take all your questions to Him. My goal for this book is to be able to increase the faith of the church. If we could all collectively rise in our faith, imagine what we could do in prayer. That is my dream for this book. So feel free to use any teaching in this book, and don't worry about giving credit. It is more important for me that the message is preached than that I would receive recognition. Now onto the final chapter of this book! You are almost done!

Builiding Your Tower

Chapter 10

The Secret to Growth

Now that you have come to the last chapter of this book, I hope that you have learned a lot and you have grown. This chapter is very special to me, as I believe that this may be the most important chapter in this book. But before we jump into this chapter, I want to tell you a little bit about how this chapter came to be.

When I started writing this book, I felt the Lord put it on my heart to write about faith. I felt like He had shown me an awesome pattern of Jesus's teachings of faith. And I never expected to even write about the Old Testament. But as the Lord was guiding me in my writing, I discovered a whole new story and aspect of faith. I got to see some old Bible stories and characters in new and interesting perspectives as the Holy Spirit taught me about faith through them. But even after all that learning and writing, I didn't actually solve the problem that I set out to solve with this book. Because the original purpose of this book isn't to teach you about faith but rather to teach you how to grow it.

So after writing all the previous chapters, I felt stuck. For the first time in the writing process, I felt like there was no real direction or answer that I could find to discover how to really grow our faith. Now in the previous chapters, I had talked about small ways to grow your faith, but many of them require some kind of faith already within you. But how do you start from zero? How do you reach the level to pray for healing when you have never seen that in your life? How do you believe in something higher when you have never had an answered prayer? So I started to pray, and God came through. After some time praying for this, which would have been a couple months of consistent daily prayer, the Lord led me to Mark 11:23.

> ***Truly I say to you, whoever says to this mountain, 'Be taken up and cast into the sea,' and does not doubt in his heart, but believes that what he says is going to happen, it will be granted him.***
>
> ***Mark 11:23***

Now this verse has to be one of the most bold and confident teachings about prayer in the Bible. It sets high standards for the things we should be able to accomplish in prayer. But this time, when I read this verse, I realized that I don't know what it means to believe in your heart. So I decided to pray that the Lord would show me what it means to believe in my heart for something. And after a couple of days of prayer, the Lord put it on my heart to seek Him for some time in isolation. So after figuring out a good couple of days to do this, I decided to separate myself from the outside world and saturated my environment with the things of God. I prayed, worshiped, fasted for some time, listened to teachings, and read my Bible. And then after this seeking, the Lord gave me my answer. He pointed me back to the fact that a person believes from their heart when they move a mountain. This seemingly small revelation led me to the parable of the sower because everything in that revelation has to do with the condition of your heart.

The Mystery of the Parable of the Sower

Now the parable of the sower is one of the most interesting and yet simple-to-understand parables that Jesus ever taught. This is, of course, because Jesus Himself gives us the explanation of the parable. So let's go over what He taught.

> *"Hear then the parable of the sower. When anyone hears the word of the*

kingdom and does not understand it, the evil one comes and snatches away what has been sown in his heart. This is the one on whom seed was sown beside the road. The one on whom seed was sown on the rocky places, this is the man who hears the word and immediately receives it with joy; yet he has no firm root in himself, but is only temporary, and when affliction or persecution arises because of the word, immediately he falls away. And the one on whom seed was sown among the thorns, this is the man who hears the word, and the worry of the world and the deceitfulness of wealth choke the word, and it becomes unfruitful. And the one on whom seed was sown on the good soil, this is the man who hears the word and understands it; who indeed bears fruit and brings forth, some a hundredfold, some sixty, and some thirty."

Matthew 13:18-23

In this parable, Jesus tells us a couple of things. One is that the seed that is being sown is the Word, and second that the field is a man's heart. This already teaches a principle that the Word of God is inherently spiritual, and it has the ability to enter into a man's heart. But the conditions of a man's heart are the most interesting aspect of this parable.

The first man's heart is one that lacks understanding. If someone comes to the Word and doesn't understand it, then the seed doesn't even enter his heart but rather it sits on the surface of the soil. This allows the devil to snatch the Word, and it never bears fruit. The second man's heart is one that does, in fact, receive the Word, but it never takes root in him. The joy that they feel comes when they realize that God is good, and His Word is good. But they don't realize either that walking in the Word brings persecution, or the truth hasn't dug deep into their heart, so it is easily burnt up by the false doctrine of the world. So when it comes time that the enemy attacks, they get burnt and give in to the pressure.

The third heart is one that is planted among thorns. This means that there were already things planted into the man's heart. Just as the Word of God can be planted into a man's heart, so also the doctrines of the world can be planted. In this case, the Word was choked out because the thorns that the world planted were choked out by worry and the lies of wealth. When you are so focused on worry and fear, you can't walk in what the Word wants you to walk in. And when you put your trust in wealth, your faith is stunted in its growth.

The last heart is the one that has had its ground broken, the rocks removed, and the thorns pulled out. It is the developed heart. And in this last heart is where we see the fruit of the Word. You see, the Word is potential, just as a seed is potential. It has the ability to radically change your life and lift you up to heights you have never been before. But why don't we see that in everyone who reads and hears the Words of God? It is because either the enemy has robbed him of the Word, or the heart of the one receiving the Word is shallow. Now two of those are from the enemy, and one is a person's responsibility. But how do we get to this place in our heart, where we can receive the Word of God, and it would bear the fruit that we desire?

Getting You to Good Soil

The good soil is obviously the goal that we all seek. The question that we are asking here is how do we move from a soil that is unfruitful to one that bears much fruit? I believe the Lord expertly laid out this parable to show us. Jesus starts with the seed that is thrown by the wayside, and there is a reason for this. This is the first condition of a man's heart. It is one that lacks understanding and one that allows the Word of God to fall flat on their heart. The basic problem here is that the person receiving the Word does not understand it. He may hear a parable, be confused, and walk away with nothing from it. But in the end, it is the man's choice to not understand because it is their decision to not seek understanding. When I was at a roadblock in this book, I could have just published the book without this chapter. It may have been a good book, but it would never have solved the problem that I was seeking to solve. It was my decision to ask the Lord for understanding. This is the first step to preparing your heart to receive the Word. It doesn't matter that you may not understand; however, it matters that you are one who seeks understanding. Always seek to understand in prayer. This is a prayer that the Lord guarantees He will answer.

> ***But if any of you lacks wisdom, let him ask of God, who gives to all generously and without reproach, and it will be given to him.***
>
> ***James 1:5***

Rocks Out and Roots Down

The second step of this process is that now that you have understanding, the Word of God has actually entered your soil. The next step is to allow the seed to put down some roots.

Previously, we talked about how when a person receives the Word, they become glad. They hear of the goodness of God, and their heart begins to change. But when persecution begins to come because of the Word, then they get burnt. Now what is really going on here? Why is it that this person, who is happy and joyful, is getting persecuted?

Well, it is because when the Word of God came into this person's heart, there was a change. That person started acting differently from the world because they received from another world; they received from God. And that Word also changed how they act or think, not just how they feel. When this starts to happen in a person, they begin to act and look separate from the world. And because of this, the world will want to persecute you. They will say that you are just acting "high and mighty," That you are just a square, That you aren't one of them. This is in the persecution that comes from the world when you have the Word in your heart.

And some people can't stand the heat. It is too much for them to bear the persecution. So they let the Word shrivel up and die in them. And it is because the Word hadn't taken root in them. It was a shallow planting. They may have had some kind of emotional response and excitement, but it didn't last. When the world rejects you, you find yourself at a fork in the road. Either you can leave your old life, old friends, and old ways of doing things, or you can return back to the ways of the world. This is decision time.

So how do we move past this point and into the next level? Well, we must allow the Word to take root and shape how we think. When we turn away from the Word, it is because we would rather avoid the present pain rather than take the future glory. But the way to move past that is to allow your heart to set its hope on the things to come, not the things of this present age. You no longer worry about what people think about you now because when you are in heaven, everyone will love you. You will have everything you need and everything you could ever want. You have to understand what has been bought for you in Christ. The second thing you will need to do is take root in a community of believers. Part of the pain of the persecution that comes is rejection. You feel rejected by the community that once loved you. And now that you are with Christ, you are rejected by them. But there is a home for you in this world, and that is the church. Find a community that loves and follows Christ and take up root there.

Pulling Out the Thorns

The last step in the process is you have to pull out the thorns or seeds that the enemy put into your heart. Jesus tells us that the thorns in a man's heart are both the deceitfulness of wealth and the worries of life. Now the worries of life could be a lot of things. It could be your career or school, your relationships, or anything else that causes you to worry. The deceitfulness of wealth, though, is an interesting one. Mind you, I would like you to note how Jesus doesn't say that wealth in itself is a thorn but rather the lies that come with wealth. Wealth is not evil, but it is rather a tool that can be used either for Satan's kingdom or the kingdom of heaven.

The problem with wealth is that if not in check, it will become a man's provision instead of God. We, as Christians, are not to live off wealth but rather the provision of God. Now this provision may come in the form of a job or career, but we are not to take that provision into our own hands. It is the way of the world to think that a man is to provide for himself. But this is false thinking. It is only by the grace of God that a man has the ability to make wealth. We should see our finances as something that God is intimately connected with. We as believers have to start to make the transition more and more out of the world system by releasing ourselves from putting provision into our own hands.

God has always provided for His people, and He always makes sure that they know it. But sometimes we forget that God is the one who brings us wealth. When we forget this basic fact of our covenant with Christ, we let worry take over our hearts. And this is when the worry of the world will come in to destroy what the Word gave you because the worries of the world are in direct opposition to the promises in the Word. God says He will take care of you, and the world says to take care of yourself. God says that you can have supernatural healing, but the world will say you are incurable. These promises that God gives you can enter your heart and bear fruit so that you are set free.

The worries of the world will also cause you to not bear fruit from the Word because part of walking and bearing fruit in the Word is you have to mix that Word with faith. You have to move in faith, and you will see fruit. But worry drowns out faith because worry is a type of fear. So you must pull out these thorns by not allowing your faith to be in money, and give your worries over to God in prayer. When you neglect prayer, you neglect God moving in your life. And when God doesn't move because you don't pray, you allow those worries to take over. God moves through prayer. This is the way that He has chosen to bless His people.

If we just assume that God will do something, and we don't pray about it, then we are misinformed. We must give ourselves over to prayer so that worry will have no foothold in our life. I remember back in 2020, I had just moved and was in a new living situation. I didn't have much money, and I only had enough money saved away for three months of rent. After those three months were up, I remember writing in my journal that I didn't have enough money to go on but that I knew God would make a way.

And over the course of those next nine months of that year, I saw God move in crazy ways. I saw Him open doors to different avenues of finances over and over again. Every time I needed help, He came through. Even if it was times where little jobs opened up, like watching someone's dog or house, or selling something online, God was always there for me. Let God have a hold of your finances, and watch Him work!

> ***Do not worry then, saying, 'What will we eat?' or 'What will we drink?' or 'What will we wear for clothing?' For the Gentiles eagerly seek all these things; for your heavenly Father knows that you need all these things. But***

seek first His kingdom and His righteousness, and all these things will be added to you.

Matthew 6:31-33 NASB1995

Reaching the Good Soil

In the last couple of sections, we went over the step-by-step process to work the soil of your heart so that it is a good place for the Word of God to grow. We talked about how we need to seek understanding, focus on the hope of the Word, find community, and live a worry-free life because we have put our trust in God, not in money. But once you get here, you get to the fun part. Now you can start to have consistent growth and change so that you can be an effective and powerful believer. When you maintain your soil, the growth of the Word becomes a natural thing. It is easy for the Word to grow but hard to maintain the cleanliness of your soil. Once you have achieved a clean soil, the next step is putting as much seed in it as possible.

You want to saturate your environment with the things of God. Listen to teachings, read your Bible, and read books about the things of God. The more you can get, the better. You can start to become a sponge for the things of God, and you can see real growth. You can start to study out things like Scriptures on healing, finances, prayer, the fruits of the Spirit, and many more. And when you study out and meditate on these Scriptures, they will enter your heart and bear fruit in your life. This fruit will lead you to apply the things you have sown into your heart. You will be able to walk in healing and pray for people to be healed. You will be able to walk in supernatural provision from God because you meditated on those Scriptures.

The Bible becomes a buffet table, where you can pick what you want to learn in that season of your life! And you can always come back for more! This has been the plan of God since the beginning, to make mankind into the image of His Son, the Word of God. If anyone today were to take everything in Scripture and have it fully bear fruit in their lives, they would look just like Jesus. That is because Jesus is the Word of God made flesh.

And the Word became flesh, and dwelt

among us, and we saw His glory, glory

> ***as of the only begotten from the Father,***
>
> ***full of grace and truth.***

John 1:14

And He paved the way so that you, too, can receive the Word and walk in it. This is one of the greatest revelations that the Lord has ever shown me, that the goal and purpose of Christ was to open a way for humanity to receive a new way of life. No longer would we live as humans, but we are called to walk as children of God. It is as if we have received a new computer code in our system, that our old code was broken and fallen, and God has given us a way to replace that
with His code, the code of the Word of God.

But How Does This Solve the Issue of Growing Our Faith?

We just went through this long deep dive into the parable of the sower, and you may be asking the question, "How does this solve the issue of growing your faith?" Well, the reason why this revelation is the path to growing your faith is because if we can get the Word of God into our hearts, then that will grow your faith. It is the number-one way to grow our faith because the Bible is full of stories of faith. If you are having a situation where you are struggling financially, you can go and sow Scriptures of financial provision into your heart. If you need healing, either emotionally, mentally, or physically, you can find Scriptures to get that healing. If you want to grow in any area, be it peace or love or joy or anything else you can think of, then you can sow that into your heart. And if you want to grow your faith, then sow Scriptures of faith into your heart. This is why Paul was able to say that faith comes by hearing and hearing by the Word of God.

> *So faith comes from hearing, and hearing by the word of Christ.*
>
> **Romans 10:17**

This whole book has been one big study of faith in the Word. If you just took everything we went through in these last chapters, studied them, and meditated on them with a clean heart, then you would grow more than you can imagine. The answer that God gave me to my question, "What does it mean to pray from your heart?" was this, that you must pray from a place where the Word has been planted in your heart. You pray from a place of revelation. Revelation is when the truth has come into your heart, and it changes you. God gave me a revelation about revelation. God has made the way easy for you to grow, and He wants you to grow. Treat the Word of God as your manual for learning how to walk as a child of God.

Praying from a Place of Revelation

When you realize that the things that have been holding you back have been your own lack of understanding, you start to develop a hunger for the Word. You realize that everything you could ever need for life is in the Word. When you study new subjects, you walk through new spiritual doors. But you need the Lord to guide you there. The doors are doorways of truth, and the Holy Spirit is the one who guides you into all truth.

> ***"I have many more things to say to you, but you cannot bear them now. But when He, the Spirit of truth, comes, He will guide you into all the truth; for He will not speak on His own initiative, but whatever He hears, He will speak; and He will disclose to you what is to come.***
>
> ***John 16:12-13***

The Holy Spirit is the one who brings a man through those spiritual doorways of revelation. And there is a very real reason why I call those doorways the doorways of truth. Because you were born into a world of lies. The foundation of how you think is framed by the lies that the devil has given you. The more doorways that you walk through, the more you leave those lies behind. You can start to walk in truth because those things you long for have already been given to you in Christ. He has bought you everything the Word has to offer. On the cross, there was a divine transaction taking place, where He was taking every punishment, and you were receiving every reward, all of this because He loves us.

So allow the Holy Spirit to sow the Word into your heart and walk through every door that is in your way. Take time to make sure your heart is good soil. I am so excited that you have finished this book and that you now have the tools to truly walk as a child of God. I hope you share this revelation with everyone you know, that God has made the way for every man to walk as His child. And that way is Jesus Christ.

> ***Jesus *said to him, "I am the way, and the truth, and the life; no one comes to the Father but through Me.***
>
> ***John 14:6***

Bibliography

"Faith Definition & Meaning." Dictionary.com. Dictionary.com. Accessed May 10, 2022. https://www.dictionary.com/browse/faith.

"G1210–Deō–Strong's Greek Lexicon (NASB95)." Blue Letter Bible. Accessed May 10, 2022. https://www.blueletterbible.org/lexicon/g1210/nasb95/mgnt/0-1/.

"G3089–Lyō–Strong's Greek Lexicon (NASB95)." Blue Letter Bible. Accessed May 10, 2022. https://www.blueletterbible.org/lexicon/g3089/nasb95/mgnt/0-1/.

"G3640–Oligopistos–Strong's Greek Lexicon (NASB95)." Blue Letter Bible. Accessed May 10, 2022. https://www.blueletterbible.org/lexicon/g3640/nasb95/mgnt/0-1/.

"G3813–Paidion–Strong's Greek Lexicon (NASB95)." Blue Letter Bible. Accessed May 10, 2022. https://www.blueletterbible.org/lexicon/g3813/nasb95/mgnt/0-1/.

"G4102–Pistis–Strong's Greek Lexicon (NASB95)." Blue Letter Bible. Accessed May 10, 2022. https://www.blueletterbible.org/lexicon/g4102/nasb95/mgnt/0-1/.

"H4603–Māʻal–Strong's Hebrew Lexicon (NASB95)." Blue Letter Bible. Accessed May 10, 2022. https://www.blueletterbible.org/lexicon/h4603/nasb95/wlc/0-1/.

"H530–'Ĕmûnâ–Strong's Hebrew Lexicon (NASB95)." Blue Letter Bible. Accessed May 10, 2022. https://www.blueletterbible.org/lexicon/h530/nasb95/wlc/0-1/.

"H539–'Āman–Strong›s Hebrew Lexicon (NASB95)." Blue Letter Bible. Accessed May 10, 2022. https://www.blueletterbible.org/lexicon/h539/nasb95/wlc/0-1/.

"H571–'Ĕmeṯ–Strong›s Hebrew Lexicon (NASB95)." Blue Letter Bible. Accessed May 10, 2022. https://www.blueletterbible.org/lexicon/h571/nasb95/wlc/0-1/.

PRINCE, DEREK. *They Shall Expel Demons What You Need to Know about Demons—Your Invisible Enemies*. S.l.: BAKER BOOK HOUSE, 2020.

Ramirez, John. *Armed and Dangerous: The Ultimate Battle Plan for Targeting and Defeating the Enemy*. United States: Baker Publishing Group, 2017.

Lewis, C. S. "Chapter 27." Essay. In *The Screwtape Letters*, 126. West Chicago, Illinois: Lord and King Associates, 1976.

Thank God for the Answer. YouTube. Warrior Notes, 2022. https://www.youtube.com/watch?v=5rcL4qX3lFs&t=12s.

CPSIA information can be obtained
at www.ICGtesting.com
Printed in the USA
BVHW031610060822
643973BV00014B/1795

9 781662 851865